THOMAS JEFFERSON at the age of 62
by Rembrandt Peale

Statute Miles

	English Settlements
	French Settlements
	Spanish Settlements

George Philip & Son, Ltd

ATLANTIC

OCEAN

Bermudas

West from Greenwich

Bahama Is.

Gulf of Mexico

New Orleans

WEST FLORIDA

EAST FLORIDA

GEORGIA

SOUTH CAROLINA

Charleston

NORTH CAROLINA

VIRGINIA

Richmond

Yorktown

Philadelphia

New York

PENN.

Pittsburg

Ohio

FRENCH LOUISIANA

Ft. St. Louis

Missouri

Mississippi

APPALACHIAN

Albany

Boston

Lexington

Massions

L. Erie

THOMAS JEFFERSON

and

American Democracy

is one of the volumes
in the

TEACH YOURSELF HISTORY
LIBRARY

Edited by A. L. ROWSE

Teach Yourself History

VOLUMES READY OR IN PREPARATION

THOMAS JEFFERSON

and

American Democracy

by

MAX BELOFF

READER IN THE COMPARATIVE STUDY OF INSTITUTIONS
IN THE UNIVERSITY OF OXFORD AND FACULTY FELLOW
OF NUFFIELD COLLEGE

Published by

HODDER & STOUGHTON LIMITED
for THE ENGLISH UNIVERSITIES PRESS
AT ST. PAUL'S HOUSE
IN THE CITY OF LONDON

First Printed 1948

PRINTED IN GREAT BRITAIN FOR THE ENGLISH UNIVERSITIES PRESS, LTD.
LONDON, BY HAZELL, WATSON AND VINEY, LTD., AYLESBURY AND LONDON

A General Introduction to the Series

THIS series has been undertaken in the conviction that there can be no subject of study more important than history. Great as have been the conquests of natural science in our time—such that many think of ours as a scientific age *par excellence*—it is even more urgent and necessary that advances should be made in the social sciences, if we are to gain control of the forces of nature loosed upon us. The bed out of which all the social sciences spring is history; there they find, in greater or lesser degree, subject-matter and material, verification or contradiction.

There is no end to what we can learn from history, if only we will, for it is coterminous with life. Its special field is the life of man in society, and at every point we can learn vicariously from the experience of others before us in history.

To take one point only—the understanding of politics: how can we hope to understand the world of affairs around us if we do not know how it came to be what it is? How to understand Germany, or Soviet Russia, or the United States—or ourselves, without knowing something of their history?

There is no subject that is more useful, or indeed indispensable.

Some evidence of the growing awareness of this may be seen in the immense increase in the interest of the reading public in history, and the much larger place the subject has come to take in education in our time.

This series has been planned to meet the needs and demands of a very wide public and of education—they are indeed the same. I am convinced that the most congenial, as well as the most concrete and practical, approach to history is the biographical, through the lives of the great men whose actions have been so much part of history, and whose careers in turn have been so moulded and formed by events.

The key idea of this series, and what distinguishes it from any other that has appeared, is the intention by way of a biography of a great man to open up a significant historical theme; for example, Cromwell and the Puritan Revolution, or Lenin and the Russian Revolution.

My hope is, in the end, as the series fills out and completes itself, by a sufficient number of biographies to cover whole periods and subjects in that way. To give you the history of the United States, for example, or the British Empire or France, *via* a number of biographies of their leading historical figures.

That should be something new, as well as convenient and practical, in education.

I need hardly say that I am a strong believer in people with good academic standards writing once more for the general reading public, and of the public being given the best that the universities can provide. From this point of view this series is intended to bring the university into the homes of the people.

A. L. Rowse.

All Souls College,
Oxford.

TO
HELEN

Preface

THE present volume had reached the proof stage before I arrived in the United States for my first visit, in the spring of this year. My visit has served to confirm in me the conviction, which I already held, that for a non-American to attempt to enter the field of American historical writing betrays some degree of temerity. Certainly this is true where the study of Jefferson is concerned, since there is possibly no period of American history upon which more scholarship is being lavished or with more promising results. This little book can do no more than try to give some idea of the present stage in Jefferson studies for the benefit of English readers. I can only crave the indulgence of those friends I have made in America into whose hands this book may come, and hope that they will regard it merely as a token of the growing interest in Great Britain in the American past in all its aspects —an interest which it is the privilege of those working in this field in British universities to try to foster as our own best contribution to the increasing mutual acquaintance of the two countries. Upon the co-operation of our American friends must depend the success of our endeavours; I have had good evidence that this co-operation is something upon which British scholars may confidently rely.

MAX BELOFF.

THE UNIVERSITY OF MINNESOTA,
 MINNEAPOLIS.
June–August 1948.

Contents

Chapter One
Introductory

IN a review of a companion volume to the present one, Sir Ernest Barker wrote that " there have been few if any great men who have been the epitomes and compendia of their age—so much one with it that to describe them would be also to describe the age." Certainly the category is a select one, but to say that no historical figures qualify for inclusion is surely an exaggeration. The career of Thomas Jefferson, and its abiding significance for an understanding of the American mind, provide at least one convincing example to the contrary. If, as Lincoln—another such figure—said, the American nation was "conceived in liberty, and dedicated to the proposition that all men are created equal," then it is hard to see how there can be a better introduction to the study of American democracy than the career of the man who most convincingly, at the time, proclaimed the conception and formulated the proposition.

But it is not simply as author of the Declaration of Independence that Thomas Jefferson can claim attention as the "epitome and compendium" of his age. On the day of the signing of that document, Jefferson had still fifty years to live—over thirty of them years of active public service, all of them years of undimmed mental vigour and undiminished intellectual influence. When the definitive

1

edition of his correspondence recently begun under the auspices of the University of Princeton is completed, it will for the first time be possible to see as a whole what may well be regarded as the most significant single contemporary commentary on one of the great formative periods of modern history. For Jefferson—intellectual progenitor of American isolationism as of so much else in modern America —was more than an American figure. His isolation sprang from no backwoodsman's ignorance of the rest of the world. Jefferson's career, on both the political and the intellectual sides, made a major contribution to what has usefully been described as "Atlantic History." And Atlantic History is, or should be, a major subject of study to all who believe in the pragmatic value of history itself.

Both from the point of view of his own country and from that of the western world as a whole, the long span of Jefferson's life covers a period truly extraordinary in the magnitude of the changes which it witnessed. Some have sought to belittle the significance of Jefferson's social and political thought by pointing out his inconsistencies and self-contradictions. But a man who could survive the American and French Revolutions, the Napoleonic era and the age of the Holy Alliance, who could live through the first great period of the industrial revolution in the Old World and of inland expansion in the New, and still retain a complete and undisturbed belief in every opinion he had ever uttered, would have out-Bourboned the Bourbons themselves in his inability to learn and to forget. Jefferson's social and political creed, formulated early in his career, was tested in action, and modified where it failed to stand the test. It is this combination of practical good sense with intellectual alertness that provides the secret of Jefferson's attraction to biographers, and makes his biography so uniquely suitable an introduction to the problems of his age.

Since the biographer cannot often turn aside to remind himself and his reader of the changing scene, it is worth lingering a moment on some of the more striking features of the age through which Jefferson lived. Thomas Jefferson was born in 1743, the year in which George II, his sovereign, personally led Carteret's "pragmatic army" of English, Hanoverian and Hessian troops into battle on behalf of Maria Theresa, against the French army which supported her rival, the Emperor Charles VII. The war, known in British history books as "the War of the Austrian Succession" and in American history books more simply and significantly as "King George's War"—as though the struggle for empire had no part in its makings—saw fighting on both sides of the Atlantic. For at the date of Jefferson's birth, the American continent and islands were the apanages of three major and two or three minor European empires.

On the mainland of America, the thirteen separate British colonies, of which Jefferson's native Virginia was one, with a population of under one and a quarter millions, faced the fifty-four thousand or so French inhabitants of New France (Canada), the still sparser population of the scattered French settlements of Louisiana which linked Canada with

New Orleans, and, to the south, the Spaniards of Florida—the outpost of an Empire which, with the exception of Portuguese Brazil and one or two lesser enclaves, stretched in unbroken majesty across the whole of the central and southern portions of the continent.

When Jefferson died in 1826, he owed no allegiance to George II's great-grandson whose ponderous bulk occupied the throne of England, nor to the seven-year-old Princess Victoria, in whose reign another and greater British Empire was to encircle the globe. Of that Empire, Canada was now part. But Louisiana and Florida were part of the United States, the American Republic. In place of the thirteen separate colonies bound together only by their common subordination to the distant imperial metropolis, a federal union now linked together twenty-four States. The frontier of settlement had reached across the mountain ranges which paralleled the Atlantic coast and beyond the Mississippi and the Great Lakes. The population of less than one and a quarter million had grown to somewhere around the eleven million mark.

To the south, the political map had undergone as sweeping a change. The empires of Spain and Portugal had collapsed, and had been replaced by a series of independent but unstable republics, and the new Empire of Brazil. Three years before his death, Jefferson had participated in the anxious consultations which led to the pronouncement known as the Monroe Doctrine, by which the United States were committed to oppose any attempt to bring Latin America under the sway of some less effete imperial power. By it also Russia was warned that the further extension southward of its Alaskan dominions, which would mean cutting short the American dream of a coast-to-coast nation, would be taken as an unfriendly act. The pattern of nineteenth-century American history stood revealed.

In Europe, the changes in Jefferson's lifetime seemed less marked. The rivalries of Bourbon, Habsburg, Romanov and Hohenzollern seemed, after the Napoleonic interlude, to be once more the dominant factors in settling the political configuration of the continent. But the resemblances were superficial—the ghost of the Revolution still stalked abroad. The dynastic disputes were less important than the bonds which united the dynasties against the disruptive forces of democracy, nationalism and socialism. The Europe of Nicholas I and Metternich was not the Europe of Louis XV and Maria Theresa. Even England, which had avoided the Revolution and had not even reformed its Parliament, was not the England of George II. The voice of Canning, who, six months after Jefferson's death, was to announce more grandiloquently than accurately that he had "called the New World into existence to redress the balance of the Old," was not the voice of Carteret.

These political changes had been accompanied by advances in technique at a rate hitherto unknown in human history. In spite of the great theoretical advances of seventeenth-century science, the world of Jefferson's birth was little advanced, as far as man's power over nature was concerned,

5

over the world of the Greeks and Romans. When Jefferson was born in 1743, Newcomen's steam-engine was the solitary harbinger of the industrial revolution and the age of steam. James Watt was seven years old, and Richard Arkwright, ten. Benjamin Franklin's experiments with electricity had not yet begun. When, less than a year before Jefferson's death, the great Erie Canal linking the Great Lakes to the Atlantic was formally opened, steamboat navigation was common on America's inland waterways, and the first experimental steamship crossing of the Atlantic lay seven years behind. The year 1826 itself saw the construction of America's first successful locomotive. If the practical conquests of electricity had yet to begin, gas-lighting was already in common use. Most significantly of all, Eli Whitney, by demonstrating the possibilities of manufacture through interchangeable parts and hence of standardized mass-production, had initiated America's own most vital contribution to technical progress, and with it, the most far-reaching of all challenges to the vital assumptions of Jeffersonian democracy. In Jefferson's own South, the eighteenth-century dominance of tobacco had given way to the reign of " King Cotton," and the nexus between southern plantation and Lancashire cotton-mill, between negro slave and English cotton-operative, was already shaping much of the social history of the nineteenth century.

Progress in the natural sciences had been accompanied by no less significant developments in other branches of thought. The years of Jefferson's youth were the high noon of French eighteenth-century philosophical and social speculation. He was five years old when Montesquieu published the *Esprit des Lois*; seven when the *Encyclopédie* began to appear; fifteen in the year of Quesnay's *Tableau Economique;* nineteen in that of *Emile* and the *Contrat Social*; twenty-one when Voltaire's *Dictionnaire Philosophique* appeared. In philosophy it was the age of David Hume. It was the age of reason and the age of scepticism.

In 1826 the age of romanticism and historicism had begun. The philosophical world was dominated by Hegel. The study of society—a unity in Jefferson's youth—was falling into its several specialisms. Adam Smith, J. B. Say, Malthus and Ricardo, whose reasoning Jefferson called "muddy," had laid the foundations of modern economics. Leopold von Ranke had published his first book, and the era of scientific history was on the horizon. Such efforts at intellectual synthesis as the new age was to make were very unlike those of the eighteenth century. Among the last to seek the intellectual patronage of Jefferson was the young Auguste Comte.

Jefferson, who had grown up at a time when the Indians of North America were the feared auxiliaries of border warfare, who was twenty at the time of Pontiac's rising—the Red Man's last great bid for freedom—lived into the time when Red Indians (except in the Far West) could be matter for romance. In the year of Jefferson's death, Fenimore Cooper published *The Last of the Mohicans*. The literary emancipation of the New World followed the consolidation of its political independence.

Of Jefferson's friends in Europe, only Lafayette,

fourteen years his junior, could claim an intimate knowledge of public affairs over so long a period. There are few conversations the historian would so like to have heard as those which took place between them when Lafayette spent a fortnight at Jefferson's home in 1824. But Lafayette was a much less interesting man than Jefferson, and one may well believe that it was the elder of the two who had the more to say.

The multiplicity of Jefferson's interests and their extraordinary range must not be allowed to obscure the essential point. What mattered most to Jefferson was none of the changes we have listed. It was the prospects of the experiment which Lafayette with his sword, and Jefferson with his pen, had helped to inaugurate a half-century earlier. Was it possible that the Americans, starting with the advantage of an almost unpeopled continent, having to fear neither overcrowding at home nor jealous enemies on every frontier, could build a society in which the great phrases of the Declaration of Independence might find fulfilment? Having got rid of kingcraft and priestcraft, of the encrusted hierarchies and traditions of the Old World, could the unaided operations of human reason contrive a society so articulated that, for the first time in recorded history, life, liberty and the pursuit of happiness might strike upon men's ears with no mocking overtones?

In his study of the Negro Problem—*An American Dilemma*—Gunnar Myrdal has described the development of American society in terms of a recurring conflict between a permanent democratic ideal and a set of facts (of which the situation of the American Negro is only one) which are clearly irreconcilable with its demands. This tension between the ideal and the real, between social theory and social fact, can be traced throughout the career and the writings of Jefferson, and the sense of tension which this communicates is what gives the Jefferson student the inescapable feeling that this eighteenth-century colonial squire is a contemporary of ours, whereas other figures of his time are not.

But this is only one side of the picture. For there was another cause which Jefferson had at heart, and which he thought to be bound up with the progress of democracy. It was the cause of peace. The war which was in progress in the year of his birth— King George's War—was only one in a series which had kept the Old World and the New World almost constantly in arms for more than half a century. Before King George's War there had been Queen Anne's War (the War of the Spanish Succession), and before that King William's War (the War of the League of Augsburg). But although the eighteenth century was a century of wars, it was also an age that cherished the dream of peace. The Abbé de St. Pierre's *Projet de Paix Perpetuelle,* published in 1713, and Kant's *Zum Ewigen Frieden,* published in 1795, indicate the persistence of this vision throughout the century. And besides these more far-reaching projects there was the steady work of the international lawyers who, while accepting the fact of war, sought to minimize its ravages by humanizing its accepted practice, and

9

by defining and fortifying the concept of neutrality. War, so Jefferson grew up to believe, was largely the product of the insensate rivalries of the monarchs and aristocracies of the Old World. The American people, masters of their own destinies, and protected against geography, could, by a wise policy of neutrality and aloofness, free themselves from the greatest scourge of mankind, and avoid both the direct impact of war and its no less deadly indirect consequences, the drain upon wealth of heavy armaments and large standing armies in time of peace. Once again the life of Jefferson reveals a tension between this instinctive view that an enlightened democracy has no need of war and the facts of his own age. For the wars which Jefferson confronted as a national statesman—the wars which began when Revolutionary France challenged the monarchs of Europe—were more continuous, more intensive, more total, in the modern phrase, than the comparatively limited wars waged by the enlightened despots of his youth. From the Marshal de Saxe to Napoleon, from Frederick II to Scharnhorst and Gneisenau, from privateering to the Continental System and the Orders in Council—the transition was not one to gladden the peace-lover. Once again the ideal and the facts clashed—in the external world and in the restless and probing mind of Jefferson. It was the same dilemma as faced two of his successors as Presidents and as leaders of the party which claims Jefferson as its founder and patron—Woodrow Wilson and Franklin D. Roosevelt. The fact that it was not Jefferson himself, but his successor and disciple, James Madison, who finally led the country into war may be regarded as largely fortuitous.

Jefferson's inconsistencies have thus a deeper explanation than the mere fact of an unusually long active career at a time of unusually rapid change. The dilemmas around which his thought revolved were permanent dilemmas. Like most of the fundamental questions of politics, they received a temporary solution, only to arise once more in a new and perhaps more acute form. It may well be that, in an imperfect world, nothing else is feasible. But even provisional solutions demand a grasp of principle. To distinguish between the transient and the permanent elements in a political creed is one of the major tasks of the political scientist, and one of the aspects of his work where the historian can be of greatest help. Unless and until the American people repudiate the Jeffersonian creed—and there is little to indicate that its vitality is exhausted— the study of Thomas Jefferson can scarcely be regarded as a purely academic exercise.

Chapter Two

Apprenticeship
(1743–1773)

PSYCHOLOGISTS tell us that character is formed in the earliest years of life, and experience suggests that the foundations of a man's beliefs, the often unconscious assumptions upon which his opinions and actions are based, are firmly fixed in most cases before the years of full maturity are reached. Nevertheless, except in the case of those few whom hereditary circumstance marks out to occupy some great place in the world of affairs, the historian can normally know but little of the formative period in the life of the men with whom he deals. For even if later fame leads to an intense interest in the early years of some great figure in the world, much of the information obtainable will be tainted by the inescapable myth-making propensities of man. Information there may be—but is it true? When a political leader is in question, the problem often extends to the early years of the subject's adult life. Except in cases of unusual precociousness, such as that of Jefferson's great rival, Alexander Hamilton, political leadership, even in an age of revolution, rarely falls to the very young. And there may be no reason at all evident to the casual observer why one young man of twenty-five or thirty rather than another, provided he belongs to the correct social stratum, should or should not attain prominence later on. The biographer can often choose between passing hurriedly over his subject's early life and embellishing it with whatever legends suit his own interpretation of the man, based upon the better-known events of his later career. Jefferson's most important biographer, Henry S. Randall, devoted only seventy-six pages to the first thirty years of Jefferson's life, out of the two thousand pages which make up the three volumes of his work which was published in 1858. Later biographers have not been averse to the other alternative—for Jefferson, a controversial figure in his own lifetime, could hardly avoid being a subject of speculation later on.

But both the sources for the study of Jefferson and those for the history of colonial Virginia have been added to since Randall's day, and historical and antiquarian scholarship have gradually made it possible to fill in some of the gaps in the conventional picture of Jefferson and his early background. As recently as 1943, Mrs. Marie Kimball, in her study, *Jefferson, the Road to Glory, 1774–1776,* made full use for the first time of the new material, to give a more adequate acount of Jefferson's early life and of the opening phases in his political career. In these materials, to quote her own words:

"The influences, social and educational, the background of family and friends which created the man that was Jefferson, spring to life. The picture of the aloof and solitary man, fond of old slippers and plain clothes, bent upon practising the democracy he was preaching, gives way to that of a gay young blade in a scarlet coat, a devoted lover, an adoring husband, a model paterfamilias, who, in his country's hour of need, revealed himself a great philosopher and an inspired public servant."

Jefferson, a great popular leader, was not himself, by birth, upbringing, or tastes, a man of the people. Indeed, as the passage just quoted shows, his early life was essentially ordinary—ordinary, that is, for a young man of the wealthy planter class of land-owners and slave-owners, who dominated the political and social scene in colonial Virginia. Jefferson was an accepted and acceptable member of a local aristocracy which, if not comparable in wealth to the great landed aristocracies of the old world, nevertheless possessed the security of inherited wealth and the confidence born of unquestioned social position.

It is true that on Jefferson's father's side the family's wealth was of comparatively recent origin, although the family had been respectably estab-lished in the colony for several generations. Peter Jefferson, his father (born in 1708), who achieved distinction as a surveyor—an important profession in an expansive agrarian society—became a man of considerable substance by wise investment and speculation in land, in the middle decades of the eighteenth century, when the wisest and most vigorous elements among the planting community were seeking opportunities to leave the exhausted tidewater lands of the original settlements for the richer soils lying towards the Blue Ridge Moun-tains. Cultivating, with the aid of a steward and five overseers, some four thousand acres, and owning other property, Peter Jefferson was, by any standard, a wealthy man, and if of little formal education, by no means devoid of intellectual interests and attainments.

Peter Jefferson's position was consolidated by his marriage in 1739 to Jane, daughter of Isham Randolph, a member of a family of the first importance in colonial Virginia and himself a public figure of some distinction. Like the Jeffersons, the Randolphs had taken part in the general movement westward, and it was from another of its members, William Randolph of Tuckahoe, that Peter Jefferson bought, in 1737, the estate in what became Albemarle County, which he named Shadwell, upon which he settled and where, on April 13, 1743, his third child and first son, Thomas, was born.

In the fragment of autobiography which Thomas Jefferson wrote at the age of seventy-seven, he tells us that his father was the third or fourth settler in that part of the country, and two years after his own birth the records show that the county contained only 106 white inhabitants, together with 177 negroes and a solitary Indian. But although an area of recent and sparse settlement, Albemarle County was not the frontier. The real frontier with its permanent defences against the Indians lay a hundred miles farther to the west, and if Jefferson had a pioneering background, his early surroundings were not those of the frontier. The group of landed families, linked by ties of friendship and marriage which formed Jefferson's social background, were intent upon reproducing as rapidly as possible the cultural life of the longer settled areas. As recent excavations have shown, Jefferson's birthplace was not a frontiersman's cabin, but a regularly planned gentleman's seat of the characteristic Virginia pattern.

The sparseness of the population of Albemarle County was not unique in Virginia, although the middle decades of the century saw a rapid influx of immigrants into the up-country. In 1756, the year before Peter Jefferson died, the population of colonial Virginia is said to have numbered 292,000, of whom 120,000 were negroes. The colony of Virginia included, as well as the modern state of that name, what are now Kentucky and West Virginia. Thomas Jefferson, in his *Notes on Virginia,* reckoned the total area at 121,525 square miles, or one-third as large again as the British Isles. If we disregard the area west of the Alleghanies as outside the range of settlement in Jefferson's youth, we get an area of about 41,000 square miles. The density of the population was about seven persons per square mile, roughly the same as that of Idaho to-day. England and Wales had, in 1756, a population of about 120 persons to the square mile.

A love of outdoor pursuits and above all of riding, a genuine sensitivity to natural beauty and, most important of all, a feeling that the good life cannot be lived except under conditions of spaciousness, that the pressure of population upon the cultivable land and hence the crowding into cities were the real causes of the perplexities and miseries of Europe—these fundamental elements in Jefferson's personality and outlook can be attributed reasonably enough to the rural surroundings of his early years.

But before that country became his home, Thomas Jefferson had had a long spell on the tidewater; for on Peter Jefferson's suddenly acquiring in 1745 the guardianship of William Randolph's orphaned son, he moved to the Randolph home at Tuckahoe, only fifty miles from Shadwell, but two or three days' hard travelling. It was here that Jefferson had his first schooling, and after the family returned to Shadwell in 1752, it was to the "Latin School" of the Reverend Mr. Douglas, at Dover Creek, some five miles from Tuckahoe, that Thomas was sent to continue his education.

In 1757 Peter Jefferson died suddenly and prematurely, and his fourteen-year-old son found himself the head of the family, which included, besides his mother, his six sisters and a baby brother. Since it was to Thomas that the lands at Shadwell and nearby now came, it was understandable that his guardians should have wished him nearer home, and Jefferson was now sent to the school conducted by the Reverend James Maury in Fredericksville Parish, about a dozen miles from Jefferson's own home. It was Maury's library, no doubt, which first gave Jefferson the entry to the world of books. And is was probably Maury who awakened in Jefferson that scientific curiosity which remained with him throughout his life.

Jefferson's interest in study was certainly sufficient for him to wish to profit by the best in that field which the colony had to offer; for we know, from his first extant letter, that it was on his own initiative that the decision was taken for him to enter the College of William and Mary at Williamsburg. He became a student there on March 25, 1760, a few weeks before his seventeenth birthday.

The college of William and Mary, founded in 1693, was junior only to Harvard among American institutions of higher education. In a community so small as eighteenth-century Virginia, the higher learning could not be too narrowly defined, and since 1727 the college had consisted of four separate "schools": a grammar school for boys up to fifteen, a philosophy school, a (post-graduate) school of divinity for fulfilling the college's original purpose of training men for the Anglican ministry, and an Indian school. The time allotted for the B.A. degree in the philosophy school was four years; but Jefferson, entering at seventeen instead of the fifteen which was apparently normal, stayed only two.

We have the testimony of one of Jefferson's contemporaries at college for his application to work during the two years which he spent there, and Jefferson's own, in his *Autobiography,* for the important influence exercised upon him by the remarkable man who directed his studies:

"It was my great good fortune, and which probably fixed the destinies of my life, that Dr. William Small, of Scotland, was then professor of Mathematics, a man profound in most of the useful branches of science, with a happy talent of communication, correct and gentlemanly manners, and an enlarged and liberal mind. He, most happily for me, soon became attached to me, and made me his daily companion when not engaged in the school;

and from his conversation I got my first view of the expansion of science, and of the system of things in which we are placed. Fortunately, the philosophical chair became vacant soon after my arrival at college, and he was appointed to fill it *per interim*; and he was the first who ever gave in that college regular lectures in Ethics, Rhetoric and Belles Lettres."

Those who have had the good fortune to come at seventeen under the influence of a first-rate teacher will hardly regard this remarkable tribute as the sentimental effusion of an old man; nor was Jefferson a sentimentalist. But apart from the tributes of his pupils, little is known of Dr. Small. His appearance on the Virginian scene was brief—appointed to his professorship in 1758, he left in 1764. His later years were spent at Birmingham, and he is known to have numbered among his friends Erasmus Darwin and James Watt.

It was through Small, as Jefferson tells us, that he met two other men who adorned the society of the tiny capital, with its two hundred houses and total population of about a thousand, including the negroes.

These two men were George Wythe, the colony's most learned lawyer, then about thirty-four years old, and Lord Fauquier, the royal lieutenant-governor since 1758, a man in his middle fifties, of considerable ability and not unenlightened views.

If these four men became, as Jefferson tells us, an inseparable "partie quarrée," it must not be imagined that Jefferson, by so much the youngest of them, was a prig, wholly devoted to the conversation and company of his elders. Fauquier instilled into him his own love of music though not his other enthusiasm, card-playing, and Jefferson became a passable performer on the violin; for the rest, he found plenty of time to follow pursuits suited to a wealthy young man of good physique and of pleasant if undistinguished appearance. Theatres, dances, racing and cock-fighting, and a first and unsuccessful romance pleasantly filled the intervals of learning. Since he clearly enjoyed an easy popularity and robust spirits, there is in Jefferson's formative years none of the darkness, the *sturm und drang*, which is so often associated in people's minds with the early lives of great men. It was a remarkably normal unclouded youth, and the only hint of something more is the fact that he did not succumb to the besetting temptations of the society of the time, that he became neither a drinker nor a gambler.

His own explanation—nearly half a century later —that he had restrained himself by asking under temptation what Dr. Small, Wythe, or his guardian Peyton Randolph would do in the circumstances— sounds too much like the conventional advice to the young to be taken at its face value; he was writing to a sixteen-year-old grandson. It seems probable that Jefferson's intellectual interests were by now sufficiently compelling for him to have the feeling that recreation, beyond that needed for health and for living a balanced and normal existence, was a waste of time and of his own talents. Furthermore, as a young man, born to a position in the world, and seeing no reason to avoid its responsibilities, Jefferson was no doubt determined to fit himself for them to the best of his ability.

By the time he left college, Jefferson's intellectual interests were fairly clearly defined. He was, in the first place, a classical scholar and, as his common-place books and later letters show, widely read in both the Greek and Latin authors. It was, as Dr. Adrienne Koch shows in her recent study, *The Philosophy of Thomas Jefferson,* upon moral teach-ings drawn from writers of both the Epicurean and Stoic schools that Jefferson based his moral creed and hence the foundation of his political attitude. In modern philosophy, the horizon was dominated by the great figure of Locke; not until a few years after leaving college did Jefferson come across the philosophical works of Bolingbroke, which may have given the impetus that led him from the ortho-dox anglicanism of his student days towards the rational deism common among his intellectual contemporaries. But the rarified atmosphere of a purely deductive system of morality was an uncom-fortable one for someone for whom moral doctrines were of importance primarily as a guide to action. And this led Jefferson, in the following years, to modify his earlier rationalism, according to the doctrines of those eighteenth-century English and Scottish philosophers who taught the doctrine of an innate moral sense. Writing to his nephew in 1787, Jefferson declared: "I think it is lost time to attend lectures on moral philosophy. He who made us would have been a pitiful bungler if He had made the rules of our moral conduct a matter of science. For one man of science, there are thousands who are not. . . . State a moral case to a plow-man and a professor. The former will decide it was well and often better because he has not been led astray by artificial rules."

But although Jefferson never lost touch with the development of philosophical thought in the narrow sense, his main interest remained in "natural philosophy," that is, in the natural and particularly the biological sciences. His interest in all that concerned geology, zoology or botany—an interest manifest in personal observations as well as in his reading and correspondence—was never purely theoretical. He was fully the child of his century in his belief that the proper study of man-kind was man, and his scientific studies led in their turn either to a consideration of human biology and human societies, or to practical applications, for instance in agriculture, which might conduce to human prosperity and hence to human felicity. There was a good deal of the utilitarian in Jeffer-son.

Similarly, mathematics, for which he seems to have had a real aptitude, was mainly valued for its statistical and topographical uses.

Although Jefferson learned to read, not only the classical languages, but also French, Spanish and Italian, and subsequently Anglo-Saxon, and although he became and remained a voracious reader, and an indefatigable collector of books, Jefferson was never particularly interested in pure literature, and rarely read novels. Philosophy, his-tory, law and politics—these were his abiding in-tellectual passions.

For a young man in Jefferson's position, the natural coping-stone to his education was some study of the law. The requirements in the way of legal knowledge exacted from an aspirant to practice in colonial Virginia were not very heavy. But if few knew much law, it was useful that many should know some law, since, as in all developing and expansive communities, disputes over property rights were frequent and complicated. Nor was the law of Virginia an easy one to master in full, consisting as it did of an uneasy compound of English common law and of imperial and local statutes as interpreted by the Courts both of the mother-country and of the colony. Here again, Jefferson was fortunate, being taken as a pupil by George Wythe, who was not merely the colony's most distinguished practitioner of the law, but in many ways its most distinguished and most learned citizen. Jefferson's studies under Wythe's direction led him beyond the daily routine of the lawyer's task to a deep acquaintance with the fundamentals of English law and of English constitutional thought. His natural mentor was Sir Edward Coke, the Whigs' oracle, whose authority was soon to be replaced in England by that of Sir William Blackstone.

In addition to the ordinary treatises and law reports, Jefferson's reading at this time included the continental writers on natural law and international law whose effects on American legal and constitutional thinking were so profound, and whose imprint on Jefferson is so well marked. The influence of the natural lawyers harmonized very

23

well with the idea (which Jefferson's philosophical studies had imparted) of the existence of a general code of moral laws, governing human society and perceptible to man. Thus Jefferson was doubly prepared for the doctrine of natural rights upon which his subsequent political creed was based. Newton and Locke, Coke and Vattel—the lines of force converged and their impact would be explosive. But there is nothing to indicate that Jefferson, busy with a huge burden of reading—some of it, as he complained, inordinately dull—methodically filling his commonplace books and summarizing cases, was in the least aware of all this.

Jefferson was admitted to the Bar at the beginning of 1767, and for the next three or four years was an active and successful practitioner, in spite of the fact that he never shone as a speaker. With the beginning of his political activities, his own practice was increasingly neglected, and Jefferson finally disposed of it to his second cousin, Edmund Randolph, in 1774.

In many respects, Jefferson's life as Wythe's pupil, and then as a practitioner on his own account, continued that of his college days. His round of social gaieties, the company of the younger members of the families who owned the nearby plantations, and, in 1766, his first journey outside Virginia which took him to Annapolis, Philadelphia, and New York—such was the lighter background to a life of study and work. His New York journey may have helped to awaken a new and absorbing interest, which dates from this period in his life, that in architecture. As early as 1767, Jefferson had determined to build a home for himself as other colonial planters were doing at the time; but there was more than a touch of originality in the choice of site. For Jefferson decided that his new house should be built on a high mountain-top overlooking Shadwell. Furthermore, there can have been few planters who took it upon themselves to design in detail their own house as Jefferson did, seemingly with the aid of an intensive study of the works of Palladio and James Gibbs. The building was begun in 1769, and a motive for hastening its completion was provided by the fire which destroyed Shadwell in the following year. But though part of Monticello was habitable by 1771, it was another decade before the building was substantially complete; and Jefferson's interest in the progress, both of the house and of the garden, to whose planning he gave equal care, was unflagging throughout.

If the building of Monticello was one sign that Jefferson now contemplated settling down upon his estates, his marriage was another. His choice for wife was Martha Wayles Skelton, who had been left a widow at the age of nineteen in 1768, and who was the daughter of a wealthy Williamsburg lawyer of English birth. Jefferson's marriage took place on January 1, 1772; he was getting on for twenty-nine. Politics apart, life seemed to have nothing but comfort and happiness to offer. But politics were apart no longer.

Jefferson's political apprenticeship had begun with his election in 1769 to the Virginia House of Burgesses. His father had also represented the county, and Jefferson's election was no more than a recognition of his social position. "As yet," wrote Edmund Randolph, "Thomas Jefferson had not attained a marked grade in politics. Until about the age of twenty-five years he had pursued general science, with which he mingled the law as a profession with eager interest and unabated thirst." Like any other young lawyer, Jefferson had attended the legislature's debates and followed its proceedings— but no more. Yet the preceding years had been remarkable in the history of Virginia, and of great significance for the future.

The form of government in Virginia was that common to most of the American colonies of Great Britain. The executive was in the hands of the royal governor and his council—that is to say, of nominees of the British Crown, controlled by instructions from Whitehall. The legislature—the House of Burgesses—which was the source of Government revenue, was elected like the English House of Commons, upon a restricted franchise, broadly representative, but giving undue weight to the planters of the original tide-water settlements. The legislative authority of the House of Burgesses was triply limited; the Governor and Council exercised a right of revision and veto as a sort of upper house; its acts were also subject to the veto of the Crown acting on the advice of a Committee of the Privy Council; and finally, its acts could be challenged on appeal in England, as repugnant to English law. Nevertheless, the history of Virginia's relations with the mother-country in recent decades had not been an unhappy one. The staple crop of tobacco found a ready outlet in Great Britain, and the mercantile regulations of the imperial Parliament did not press as hardly upon its economy as upon those of the colonies farther north. It is true that reliance on a staple crop had had its usual effects in binding the planters firmly by ties of debt to the English merchants who bought their crop and supplied their needs; and this perennial indebtedness was increased by the credit facilities offered to the planters to enable them to meet the expenditure demanded by their rising standards of living and culture. But on the whole, the Government and the dominant planter-class stood together.

For the real division in colonial Virginia was, and had been since the late seventeenth century and Nathaniel Bacon's abortive rebellion in 1676, a conflict within the colonial society itself, between the larger planter of the tide-water and the up-country farmer, who was often his debtor. The social cleavage was strengthened by religious divergences, since, while the planters adhered to the established church, many of the new-comers to the back-country, particularly those from Scotland, Ulster and continental Europe, belonged to the Presbyterian, Baptist or other minor sects. Although religious toleration had been granted to the former as early as 1699, the dissenters were still taxed for the upkeep of a Church the proportion of whose adherents in the colony's population was steadily declining.

The history of Virginia in the eighteenth century had been, from one point of view, one of an unswerving attempt by the tide-water planters to hold and consolidate their supremacy, to ignore the claims of frontiersmen and squatters, to control production, trade, and the allotment of new land for settlement in their own interests, and to impose the maximum of religious uniformity. The hostility which this engendered in the up-country at times more than counterbalanced the common interests which all classes in the colony possessed as against the home Government, such as the fact that all Virginians desired to keep suits for debt brought against them by Englishmen in the colonial courts and all wished to avoid the quit-rents payable to the Crown. Nevertheless, the line between parties was not an immutable one and did not coincide with a simple geographical division. As the story of the Jeffersons shows, the Piedmont was essentially an extension of the tide-water civilization; the true frontier lay beyond.

In the years preceding Jefferson's entry into politics, Patrick Henry, a man of scant education but an outstanding orator, had sprung into prominence as leader of the Scotch-Irish, the most important element among the western settlers. He had come to the front at the age of twenty-seven in an affair known as the "parson's cause." The Virginia Assembly passed a law to prevent the clergy of the established church, whose salaries had hitherto been calculated in tobacco, from profiting by a heavy rise in its price. This Act was in 1760 disallowed by the Crown. Jefferson's old tutor, Maury, was one of those who brought a suit for the extra amount. In response to Henry's assertion that the Crown had no right to disallow the Act and that its action was a breach of the compact between Great Britain and her Colonies, the County Court awarded the minister only nominal damages, thus challenging both the authority of the established church and the support from Britain upon which it relied.

The rise of new political leaders in Virginia coincided with a far-reaching crisis in the affairs of the American colonies as a whole. Some such development was perhaps bound to occur, as the colonies grew in strength and vigour and became more conscious of their interests as separate communities. The authority of the Crown, exercised through separate British departments, proved increasingly irksome. But the limitations on colonial autonomy which it imposed had the sanction of long custom, while it was usually possible for the royal representatives to work hand in hand with the wealthier colonists. In many respects, the objects for which the Crown worked—to limit the pace of inland expansion so as to protect the Indians and, with them, the fur trade; to maintain colonial credit by preventing the issue of paper currency; to preserve the slave trade from Africa—were objects which the ruling elements in the colonies accepted or even welcomed. But in most colonies, the subordination of colonial trade to the requirements of the British tariff and navigation Acts was seriously resented, especially as the administration of these laws was progressively tightened. The advantage of the guaranteed markets which the colonies enjoyed within the imperial system was partly offset by the declining profits from tobacco after 1750. Finally, the prohibition in the colonies of certain branches of industry was a matter of growing concern.

The reasons which caused the ultimate breakdown of a system which seemed solid enough when Jefferson went up to William and Mary in 1760 are complex, and historians still find it hard to agree about the relative importance of the different forces at work. It is fairly clear that the growth of the colonies was accompanied by changes in the form of British government which laid bare the empirical foundations of the imperial system, and produced clashes which only some clearly accepted principle of association could be relied upon to solve. The original premise that all the inhabitants of the colonies were subjects of the British Crown as their ancestors had been became less self-evident as the exclusively English population of the original settlements were subjected to dilution. But at this stage the more important fact was that, as British subjects, the inhabitants of the colonies were expected to acknowledge the authority of the British Parliament, an assembly in which they had no voice. The events of the second half of the seventeenth century had decisively altered the character of the British constitution, and by the middle of the eighteenth century the sovereignty of Parliament was an unchallenged dogma of British political thought. The colonists who had had no share in the Glorious Revolution or its sequel, who regarded their Governments as limited by express or implied compacts with the Crown, could not be expected to accept this change without question, once serious matters of disagreement had arisen. The assumption that the British constitution, as it now stood, was a part of the divine order, and that all was well, since the policies of Parliament were designed to benefit the Empire as a whole, was easier to accept in Britain than in America. In one respect the failure of imperial policy had been complete. Not only had the colonists, even in time of war, been reluctant to discuss their interests from the point of view of the Empire as a whole, but they had on the whole been unwilling to take a point of view wider than that of each individual colony. Here the revolutionary movement was to succeed where the imperial administration had failed.

There were two results of the colonies being subordinate in fact if not in theory to a Parliamentary majority, and to an administration dependent upon it. In the first place, the colonists felt that their interests were subordinated where policy was concerned to the requirements of Parliamentary strategy and too much influenced by the wiles of powerful "lobbies" at Westminster. In the second place, there was the fact that politics was first and foremost a question of jobs, and that the overlapping of the British departments concerned made American patronage a particularly happy hunting-ground for those in search of places for needy relatives or clients. Nothing did more to disgust Americans with the imperial connection than the thought that the colonies were being used as a dumping-ground for the less competent members of the British ruling class.

Until 1756 the centrifugal tendencies inherent in this situation were largely checked by the fact that the colonies relied upon the imperial Government for their defence in time of war. But with the renewal in that year of the Anglo-French conflict, the position on the North American continent underwent a rapid change. In 1758 the great fortress of Louisburg fell to the British, and in 1759 Quebec itself was captured. By the Peace of Paris in 1763, Canada and Cape Breton Island were ceded to Great Britain by France, and Florida by Spain. In compensation for Florida, Spain received from France the vast empty territory of Louisiana west of the Mississippi and a strip of land east of its delta. The menace of French encirclement had disappeared.

The relations between Great Britain and her original colonies now depended upon the disposition she made of her conquests and the manner in which she reimbursed herself for their cost. Both these problems were handled in such a way as to cause widespread disaffection in America. The problem of dealing with the lands between the existing frontier of settlement and the Mississippi was complicated by the conflicting claims of various colonies arising from the uncertain topography of the early charters. Virginia itself claimed land reaching right up to the Mississippi itself, and various Virginians, including George Washington and the Lees, were interested in projects for settlement there. Other land companies with English and American members were also pressing claims. But British ministers were disinclined to regard the further opening up of the interior as an advantage. They wanted settlers of British stock for Nova Scotia and for Florida, and they were afraid that settlers in the American west would be neither profitable customers nor disciplined subjects. It would be better to leave the Indians in possession and to encourage the fur trade of Britain's newly acquired Canadian subjects, whose economy, like their domestic institutions, would thus remain substantially undisturbed.

The Indian rising under Pontiac in 1763 showed that the Indian danger was no figment of the imperial Government's imagination. Its immediate result was the Proclamation of October 1763, by which the western lands were removed from the control of the colonial governors and by which settlement was prohibited west of the Alleghany watershed. This was intended to be a temporary expedient to enable a new policy to be worked out at leisure, and there were projects for the creation of new colonies from which the British Government hoped for eventual revenue in the shape of quitrents. But the changes in the ministry at London prevented anything being done; and the temporary endured. Meanwhile, the energies of the land companies were still further devoted to winning political support in England, although Washington, believing that the 1763 settlement could not last, advised his fellow-Virginians to continue staking their claims. The adoption, in 1768, of a new Indian policy providing for an Indian boundary line which was only gradually to be moved westward, and for the purchase of Indian lands only through the medium of agents of the imperial Government, confirmed the feeling that Virginia's western interests were being sacrificed to merchants and speculators in the middle colonies and at home. Britain's intention appeared to be to close up all possibilities of alternate investment for the inhabitants of the tobacco colonies, and to confine them to single-crop production for the benefit of their British creditors.

On the financial side it was felt in London that the burdens of the war had fallen too exclusively upon the home taxpayer, and Pontiac's rising seemed to indicate the necessity of maintaining a permanent force in the colonies which would also involve expense. Two measures were therefore adopted. The Sugar Act of 1764 imposed new taxes upon colonial trade, and while reducing the amount of the molasses duty—one of the most important burdens on the colonies' imports—made provision for its more efficient collection. The Stamp Act of 1765 imposed a series of stamp duties upon a wide range of legal and commercial documents, and on newspapers, almanacs, pamphlets, and playing-cards. In addition to the financial burden on individual traders, these measures would, so it was felt in the colonies, aggravate the colonies' persistent lack of specie and consequent inability to pay for imported goods, since the proceeds of the new taxes would be transferred to Britain in cash and expended there. While all the colonies were affected by these two Acts, Virginia had a separate grievance in the Currency Act of 1764, which forbade her to continue the practice of making the colony's bills of credit legal tender, and which compelled her to withdraw from circulation those issued during the war.

Such were the opportunities which British policy provided for the demagogue of genius who now dominated the Virginia legislature. The older leaders of the House of Burgesses were content to let the matter rest with a dignified petition against the Stamp Act. But in May 1765, towards the end of the session, and in an exceptionally thin house, Patrick Henry, in a speech which verged upon the treasonable, put forward a series of resolutions which unequivocally declared that the principle of the British constitution was that no man should be taxed but by his own representatives, and that Virginians were obliged to pay no taxes other than those laid upon them by their own Assembly. Powerful figures like John and Peyton Randolph and George Wythe opposed the use of extreme language, and urged that the colony should await a reply to the conciliatory petition of the preceding year. But Henry, supported by R. H. Lee and the votes mainly of the Piedmont members, succeeded by narrow majorities in carrying five of the seven resolutions he had drafted, although one was later rescinded. All seven were published in the colonial press, as though the Virginia Assembly had passed them, and the radical leaders thus acquired an audience and a reputation throughout the colonies.

The later events in the crisis saw the centre of interest pass from the plantation colonies to New England, and Virginia was not represented in the Stamp Act Congress—an intercolonial conference— at New York in October 1765. In March 1766, the Stamp Act was repealed as a result of the fierce colonial opposition, and of pressure from London merchants interested in American trade, which was being hard hit by a colonial boycott. At the same time a Declaratory Act was passed which expressly repudiated the doctrines which Patrick Henry had proclaimed, and asserted the right of Parliament to "bind the colonies in all cases whatsoever." The intentions of Parliament were more fully revealed in the following year, when, in deference to the distinction some colonial writers had made between Parliament's right of regulating trade by external taxes and its wrongful claim to levy internal taxes in the colonies, Charles Townshend introduced a new series of import duties out of which were to be paid the salaries of colonial governors and judges, as well as the expenses of colonial defence. By this means the political control which command of the purse had given the colonial legislatures would be seriously impaired. Once more a wave of protest swept through the colonies.

The initiative was taken by Massachusetts. Its legislature, in January 1768, sent a petition to the British Government protesting against the new duties, and at the same time sent a circular letter to the other colonies inviting their support. This letter met with a favourable response from the Virginia Assembly when it met on March 21, and a circular letter from that body was sent to reinforce the Massachusetts plea. The British Government decided to take severe measures, and the Massachusetts Assembly was ordered to rescind the circular letter. Its refusal to do so was followed by its dissolution. A further inroad upon what the colonists regarded as their prescriptive right of self-government was the suspension in 1767 of the legislative privileges of the New York Assembly, in consequence of that colony's refusal to provide the supplies called for by the Quartering Act of 1765.

The British view was that the rights of Parliament in the colonies were in no way affected by the existence of local representative institutions. Their authority, it was implied, could only derive from that of Parliament itself, and was consequently always subject to recall. The appointment of a new American Board of Commissioners of the Customs, and a strengthening of the authority of the Admiralty Courts, were additional indications of the fact that British policy was working towards the concept of a centrally governed and administered empire against which local interests and privileges would count for little.

On the other hand, the movement to resist the British measures was far from commanding universal adherence. Protests had availed nothing, and the obvious course to adopt was that of an economic boycott, since this was likely to cause the British ministry the most trouble at home. The radical politicians in the New England and Middle colonies did their best to organize the colonial merchants for this purpose, and agreements not to import British goods were entered into between March 1768 and March 1769, by the merchants of Boston, New York, Philadelphia and other towns, although not without a good deal of opposition, particularly from the wealthier inhabitants. There were radical demonstrations, not only against British officials, but against those elements in the colonial population which seemed lukewarm in what was increasingly coming to be regarded as the national cause, and was so presented in the mainly radical or patriot press. Indeed, the unconcealed desire of at least some of the supporters of the non-importation agreements to use them as a means of stimulating local industry, so as to make the colonies economically independent of Britain itself, was so obviously contrary to the idea of a single, united, self-sufficient empire which had been the previous foundation of their economic life, that vested interests were bound to be adversely affected. The choice which had to be made was not simply one affecting the future relations of the colonies and the mother-country; it was bound to determine to a large extent the future internal evolution of the colonies themselves. The conservative opposition to the non-importation movement could also be adhered to on less egocentric grounds. The use of economic sanctions, especially when backed up by talk of colonial self-sufficiency, was bound in the long run to lose the Americans most of their supporters in England. The British Government would then have the support which it needed in order to take strong measures. Similarly, attempts to provoke the British Government into further measures of repression, by interfering, for instance, with the collection of customs, were two-edged in their results. They helped to keep the excitement at fever-pitch in the colonies, but they discouraged the parliamentary advocates of conciliation. Even those British politicians who most strongly attacked the Government's measures on the grounds of expediency never accepted the constitutional arguments by which the colonists justified their resistance. The more the colonists stood on their "rights," the less the chance that they would receive a hearing for their practical grievances.

When Jefferson attended the opening of the new session of the House of Burgesses on May 8, 1769, the moment was an important one in the affairs of Virginia as well as in Jefferson's own career. Jefferson was appointed to the Committee for drawing up an address in reply to the speech of the new Governor, Lord Botetourt, and to the Committee for Privileges and Elections. Jefferson, who had some reputation as a writer, was asked to draft the resolutions which it was customary to pass as heads of the address, as well as the address itself. The resolutions, which were accepted by the House, contain, as their only reference to recent events, the assurance that if any matters should arise affecting the interests of Great Britain, they should be discussed on "this ruling principle that her interests and ours are inseparably the same." But Jefferson's draft address, rather to his mortification, was not accepted by the Committee.

These were all only preliminaries. The real point at issue was the attitude which Virginia was going to take towards the non-importation agreements. On May 16 the Assembly passed four resolutions which declared again that the sole right of taxing the inhabitants of Virginia was legally and constitutionally vested in the House of Burgesses, that it was their undoubted privilege to petition the Crown for a redress of grievances and to join with other colonies in so doing, and that all trials for treason should be held within the colony, and not removed to British courts, as had been proposed in a recent resolution of the British Parliament, suggesting the revival of a long-disused law of Henry

VIII. It was also resolved that the last of these points should be incorporated in a petition to the Crown, and that the resolutions themselves should be circulated to the Assemblies of the other colonies for their concurrence. This open defiance of the British Government led, as might have been expected, to the dissolution of the House.

The great majority of the members of the dissolved House of Burgesses met in a tavern on the following day and drew up a non-importation agreement—published as the Virginia Association. This document, drafted by George Mason and signed among others by George Washington, Patrick Henry, R. H. Lee and Jefferson himself, exhausted the immediate radical urge, and the proceedings ended with loyal toasts. The Association was widely endorsed, but there was significant opposition from some of the larger planters and from the merchants, who were for the most part agents of British firms. On the other hand, the cessation of imports gave a useful opportunity for economy and retrenchment to those planters who were heavily burdened with debt after what had been a period of considerable commercial depression.

The subsequent elections to the House of Burgesses confirmed the public support for those members who had adopted the Association, and there was soon evidence that the British Government was still prepared to try the path of conciliation. The House was again convened on November 7, 1769, and were informed by the Governor that the British Ministry proposed to remove the Townshend duties, other than that on tea, and that no design was entertained by them, or had been, to lay further taxes upon the Americans for the purpose of raising revenue.

For the remainder of the Session, which lasted until December 21, the Assembly was occupied with domestic problems. This gave Jefferson the opportunity of acting in committee as seconder of a motion designed to facilitate the manumission of slaves. The Committee proved exceedingly hostile to the idea, and disposed rather to strengthen the slave code than to liberalize it. Not for the last time Jefferson found himself at odds with the prevailing sentiment on the subject of the negroes.

The next three years were years of comparative calm. The clash with British troops at Boston in March 1770, which propaganda dignified and magnified as the Boston Massacre, helped to convince the merchants everywhere that the power of the mob was growing too great, and that their legitimate grievances were being exploited for political ends. New York was the first colony to denounce the non-importation agreement, and its enforcement was widely allowed to lapse. The promised repeal of the Townshend duties took place, and that on tea, which was retained largely as a symbol, was either quietly paid or even more quietly evaded. By the spring of 1772 the radical movement seemed a spent force.

But the apparent calm and the triumph of the moderates were alike illusory. The clash between the colonists and the British Parliament ran deeper than particular economic grievances. The ultimate issue was a political one—where did sovereignty in the colonies lie? Until that was decided, a permanent settlement could not be reached.

The fact that these considerations were by now strongly present in Jefferson's mind may perhaps be surmised from the interesting evidence we have of his sudden preoccupation with the study of political science. A list of fourteen books shipped to him from a London bookseller in September 1769 is entirely devoted to parliamentary history and procedure and to works on government and political history. It included three items of considerable significance to the student of Jefferson's political thought: Burlamaqui's work on natural law, Locke and Montesquieu. Of these, to judge from his commonplace book, it was the *Esprit des Lois* which gave Jefferson most food for thought. There is no reason to believe that he did not at this time share the general American enthusiasm for the work or had yet arrived at his later critical attitude towards many of Montesquieu's leading ideas.

The period of domestic bliss and quiet study which Jefferson now enjoyed was soon ended by the renewal of political strife. The ground for this had been prepared by the restless propagandist and organizing activities of Samuel Adams of Massachusetts, whose Committees of Correspondence were used to build up an organized political party ready to exploit the next clash both against the home Government and against those elements in America who were insufficiently forward in the struggle. The first overt incident was provided by the destruction of a revenue vessel off the Rhode Island coast in June 1772. This was followed by the establishment of a special commission to seek out suspects, and arrange for their transfer to England for trial—tasks which the hostility of the inhabitants made impossible of fulfilment.

In 1772 Jefferson had failed altogether to attend the House of Burgesses, but when it next met, on March 4, 1773, he was again in his place.

He at once figured among the active leaders on the radical side in the Assembly, and as such shared the responsibility for the resolutions presented on March 12, which included the appointment of a "standing committee of correspondence and inquiry." Jefferson's name stood last on the list of its eleven members. The Committee acted as directed by the Assembly, communicating to the Assemblies of the other colonies the Virginians' anxieties about the reported threats to their ancient, legal and constitutional rights, and suggesting that the other Assemblies appoint similar committees. On this occasion the Governor's reaction was less drastic and the session was allowed to continue for another eleven days. The House was then prorogued, and was not recalled until May 5, 1774.

By this time the American scene had darkened. The British Government, in an effort to make the tea duty a reality, and to help the powerful East India Company out of its financial embarrassments, had passed a new Act remitting the entire duty on tea re-exported to America and allowing the Company itself to engage directly in the trade. The loss which this threatened to American merchants, and the probability that the tea would find purchasers despite the tax, since the Dutch smugglers could

43

now be undersold, united smugglers, merchants and radical patriots in a common determination to resist its importation. In Boston, feelings were already high because of the recent publication, by the radicals, of the correspondence of Governor Thomas Hutchinson, which contained expressions capable of being interpreted as a threat to American liberties. And it was Boston which took the lead. On December 16, 1773, three shiploads of the offending tea were seized by gangs of patriots disguised as Red Indians, and thrown into the harbour. The "Boston Tea-Party," which was imitated in other ports, was the most direct challenge, so far, to the authority of the imperial Government. It was a challenge which could not be ignored, and which few in England would have wished the Government to ignore. On March 25, 1774, a Bill, closing the port of Boston to all commerce until the citizens had indemnified the Company and the revenue officers concerned, and given adequate evidence of their future good intentions, passed the House of Commons without a division. On May 11, 1774, the news of the Boston Port Act reached Boston. The American Revolution had begun.

Chapter Three

American Independence
(1774–1776)

THE dramatic series of events which began with the Boston Tea Party and ended with the Declaration of Independence form a familiar pattern, so familiar indeed that even the most wary of historians is all too likely to take it for granted that a total separation of the colonies from Great Britain and the birth of a new American nation were implicit in the political situation at the end of the third quarter of the eighteenth century. The story of the Revolution itself, as it unfolded before the eyes of contemporaries, was far more complex, indeed, far more confused, than might be imagined from later accounts. Like so much else which had taken place or was to take place on the American scene, the Revolution had no obvious precedent. There had been in the past risings of people against tyrants, and the great volumes in which John Rushworth had collected the records of the struggle against Charles I were diligently perused by those seeking for constitutional precedents. It was not for nothing that the first American warship was to be named the *Oliver Cromwell*. But previous movements of rebellion had been concerned with the redress of grievances and the establishment of reformed modes of government within an existing state. Where the rebellion had been

45

against a foreign tyrant—as with the Dutch rising against Philip II of Spain—the rebels could look back to a previous condition of independence and native rule to set against a newly imposed servitude.

But in the present case the Americans were following an uncharted path. They had no political status other than as members of particular communities within a powerful and successful empire. The communities to which they belonged had no tradition of common action, and in default of adequate communications had little possibility of drawing much closer together. Their numbers had, it is true, recently increased—perhaps doubled since Jefferson's birth. Estimates put the total population at about 2,200,000 in 1770, and about 2,780,000 a decade later. Between those two dates, Virginia passed the half-million, and Pennsylvania, Massachusetts and North Carolina the 300,000, mark. But even in 1780, Maryland had barely a quarter of a million inhabitants, and New York and Connecticut a mere 200,000. In reckoning the real strength of these communities, it must further be taken into account that, of the two and a half million Americans at the time of the Revolution, half a million were slaves, and that in Virginia they made up two-fifths of the entire population.

Again, the colonies had few of the urban agglomerations which might stimulate political consciousness and the habit of active co-operation for public ends. Only five American towns had populations of more than 12,000 in 1774: Philadelphia, with 40,000—the intellectual as well as the commercial metropolis of colonial America; New York, with 25,000 to 30,000; Boston, with 20,000; Charleston and Newport, with about 12,000 each. The next largest town in the South, Baltimore, had about 6,000 inhabitants. Neither Virginia nor North Carolina could boast one so large. Of the five major urban centres, all except Charleston, with its unique urban-rural planter society, depended for their livelihood on their trade with Great Britain. In that respect the authors of the Boston Port Bill had calculated correctly.

Furthermore, as the economic history of the early years of independence was to show, the economic pattern of colonial society was affected only on its fringes by the fact of political subordination. The position of the American colonies as suppliers of raw materials for Great Britain itself, and of food and other supplies for her tropical colonies, was the necessary consequence of a scanty population, a lack of capital and of the institutions necessary to mobilize it, and of economic conservatism. Americans, indeed, very largely ignored the tremendous strides made by Great Britain in agricultural and industrial technique. None of the weaknesses in the American position was removed or could be removed by the mere assumption of political independence. In some respects, indeed, exclusion from the Empire was certain to enhance rather than to diminish the economic difficulties of the colonies. For their exclusion from trading freely with other countries was not solely the result of British mercantilism—the economic doctrines of the first British Empire were paralleled by still more restrictive doctrines and practices in the rival empires of France and Spain.

Even the obstacles placed by the imperial Government in the way of western expansion could be justified by pointing out the very great difficulties which the colonies had always found in combating the Indians with nothing but their own resources.

For these reasons the enumeration of economic grievances should not be taken as equivalent to an analysis of the causes of the revolution. The economic arguments for reconciliation were, as many contemporaries perceived, at least as powerful as those in favour of resistance. To suggest that the merchants revolted so as to secure access to more markets, or the planters so as to free themselves from the burden of their debts, is to ignore important aspects of the situation and the lessons which may legitimately be drawn from the study of other revolutionary movements.

We who have witnessed the rise and triumph of national movements inside and outside Europe surely need no reminding how slender a bond of political union are the ties of economic or indeed political self-interest. There comes a point, it appears, where every community becomes sufficiently aware of its own psychological self-sufficiency for the idea of subordination to seem intolerable, at least to a vocal and active minority, where the political tenets of the age acquire a new meaning as instruments of action. If such a minority finds a resolute leadership, the hesitations of the majority can be ignored, and active opposition cowed into submission by the threat of physical violence. Such a leadership will know how to exploit the internal stresses of the community so as to drive home its advantage, to identify conservatism with privilege, privilege with reaction, and reaction with treachery to the national cause.

The leaders of the American revolution—a coalition drawn from the two wholly dissimilar societies of Virginia and Massachusetts—rank first among the exponents of this technique. In spite of the physical obstacles which the geography of the colonies placed in their way, their success in building up the revolutionary movement was astonishingly complete and rapid. This success they owed in great measure to the fact that they had themselves been active members of communities which in their limited and parochial way were real schools of self-reliance and self-government. The mechanism of political action and the practice of ordered government were no novelty to them. In spite of the coercion which they applied to their political opponents, and of the inevitable excesses with which this was accompanied, the leaders of the American revolution never lost control, either of themselves, or of their following. In the second place, they owed their success to the wide appeal made by the political creed with which they justified their appeal to arms. Some British historians of the period—such as Francis W. Hirst, the author of an outstanding biography of Jefferson—have argued that the animus against Great Britain which Americans writing of this period still show is unjustified because the British people as a whole were not opposed to the American cause. But on this point George III and

Lord North certainly represented the feelings of most of the elements in British society which found representation in the eighteenth-century Parliament. As we have seen, once the issue of sovereignty became uppermost, it was hardly possible that the point could be conceded. The radicals who continued to sympathize with the Americans were a minority. But their influence was important, and it was certainly of great consequence to the future of British institutions that these should be criticized for their unrepresentative character, that their title-deeds should be scrutinized by the light of reason, and that prescription should be rejected as a foundation of political obligation. It is a literary rather than an historical decision which leads us to study Burke and neglect Tom Paine. Of equal significance was the intellectual impact of the American revolution upon continental Europe, and in particular upon France.

These far-reaching repercussions of events in the distant dependencies of the British Crown were due partly to the simple fact that the colonists won that part of the struggle which can properly be termed the War of American Independence, and partly to the genial fashion in which their cause was presented to the world. For the first of these facts—the fact of victory—they were indebted to the military and political abilities of George Washington and to the accident of French support; for the second, they were indebted primarily to another Virginian—Thomas Jefferson. With the meeting of the Virginia House of Burgesses in May 1774, the period of Jefferson's political and intellectual apprenticeship came to an end, and in the course of the next two years he was to have ample opportunity of displaying both his capacity for political action and his ability as a propagandist.

The early meetings of the session were marked by no special feature, and the ordinary business of the House was transacted quietly. It was the news of the Boston Port Act which was the signal for action. As before, the radical group, Jefferson, Patrick Henry, Richard Henry Lee, and a few others, took the lead in insisting that Virginia make common cause with Massachusetts. It is clear that, for a great many people in Virginia, a community of interest with the distant New Englanders was by no means self-evident. It was necessary to persuade them that the punitive measures against Boston were part of a general plot for the extirpation of American liberties. To do this, a device was hit upon for which Jefferson was at least partly responsible; this was the use of the pulpit as a weapon of propaganda by the proclaiming of a day of fasting and prayer. Robert Nicholas Carter—one of the most conservative of the burgesses and chairman of the committee on religion—was persuaded to move the necessary resolution, which was at once adopted. Although the resolution was by no means revolutionary in tone, the challenge was not one which the Governor could ignore, and on May 26 the Assembly was duly dissolved.

The procedure of 1769 was resorted to again. The Burgesses met at the Raleigh Tavern, adopted a new Association for restricting trade with Britain, and proposed that a general Congress of deputies from all the Colonies should meet at Philadelphia on September 5, to consider further measures. Meanwhile, a special Convention was to be elected for Virginia, to choose delegates to the general Congress, and to instruct them upon their course of action.

The day of prayer, which was duly observed on June 1, seems to have had its intended effect, and the new Convention was composed of the members of the old Assembly, who could thus claim popular approval for their past actions and a mandate for the future.

Jefferson himself was elected for Albemarle County, and the freeholders assembled for the election also passed a series of resolutions whose language and content leave little doubt but that Jefferson himself was their author. It was indeed typical of Jefferson's approach to political problems that the resolutions began with a statement of general principles which went beyond the matter actually at issue:

"*Resolved,* That the inhabitants of the Several States of British America are subject to the laws which they adopted at their first settlement, and to such others as have since been made by their respective Legislatures, duly constituted and appointed with their own consent. That no other Legislature whatever can rightly exercise authority over them; and that these privileges they hold as the common rights of mankind, confirmed by the political constitutions they have respectively assumed, and also by several charters of compact from the Crown."

For Jefferson, therefore, there was no need to limit the argument to the legal interpretation of colonial charters and precedents: the basis of the colonists' claim to self-government lay in the natural right of every man to be governed only by his own consent. The legal forms of the self-governing institutions of the American colonies —or States as Jefferson here calls them—merely register and confirm these natural rights. It was on this high level that the argument proceeded:

"*Resolved,* That these their natural and legal rights have in frequent instances been invaded by the Parliament of Great Britain and particularly that they were so by an act lately passed to take away the trade of the inhabitants of the town of *Boston,* in the province of Massachusetts Bay; that all such assumptions of unlawful power are dangerous to the rights of the British empire in general, and should be considered as its common cause, and that we will ever be ready to join with our fellow-subjects in every part of the same, in executing all those rightful powers which God has given us, for the re-establishment and guaranteeing such their constitutional rights, when, where, and by whomsoever invaded."

The resolutions went on to advocate a complete severance of commercial relations with Great Britain until the Boston Port Act should be repealed, together with all Acts laying taxes or restrictions upon American trade, and those prohibiting or restraining internal manufactures.

Jefferson himself was prevented by sudden illness from attending the Virginia Convention, nor was his name among those of the seven delegates which it appointed to represent the colony at Philadelphia. But his opinions were in no danger of being ignored, since he had sent along two copies of a document which he intended should be adopted as instructions for the delegates to the general Congress. Although this document was not officially brought to the notice of the Convention, it was read to a private meeting by Peyton Randolph.

Like the Albemarle resolutions, the proposed instructions took up a position much more extreme than that generally adopted at the time either in Virginia or the other colonies, since most people were still prepared to accept the authority of Parliament in all matters other than taxation, and to admit its right of general legislation for the welfare of the empire. The argument from natural rights was too bold and too much outside the ordinary range of political discussion for it to be accepted at once as the basis of the colony's claims. The document was, however, printed forthwith under the title: *A Summary View of the Rights of British America*. The author's name was not given, but there was no attempt to conceal it; and Jefferson's national reputation may be said to date from its publication.

The *Summary View* is indeed a remarkable document, if one remembers the date of publication. It shows how firmly established was Jefferson's political philosophy, and the use to which he had put his political studies. These had lately ranged over large tracts of ancient, mediæval and modern history in an effort to establish the nature and origins of kingship and, with them, its proper limits; as well as the contractual origins of government, and hence the rights of secession and rebellion.

But the assumption that Jefferson's views were the result of his reading, that the *Summary View* is the product of meditations upon Locke, or Algernon Sydney, or Vattel, is to misconceive the process of political creativity. It is not the premises, but the conclusions that matter, in a piece of writing which is intended to have practical results. The conclusions were driven home to Jefferson by the facts of the political situation as he saw it; his task was to provide the premises from which these conclusions could most cogently be argued, and to convince himself and his readers that a theory of the imperial constitution which was entirely novel was in harmony with their experience and their normal modes of thought.

The *Summary View* begins with an appeal to the King to give attention to the representations now made by his American subjects:

"And this his Majesty will think we have reason to expect when he reflects that he is no more than the chief officer of the people, appointed by the laws, and circumscribed with definite powers, to assist in working the great machine of government, erected for their use, and consequently, subject to their superintendence."

This notion of limited monarchy, even if expressed with unusual bluntness, did not of course go beyond the Whig theory as generally accepted in England since the Revolution of 1688-9.

It is when Jefferson proceeds to consider the relations of England with the colonies that the novelty of his position becomes apparent. For the British colonies in America had been established through the exercise by free Britons of their natural right of expatriation and of setting up new societies under such laws and regulations as seemed to them "most likely to promote public happiness." Happiness as the object of government—the note was a new one. The parallel to this colonizing movement was found by Jefferson in the Anglo-Saxon conquest of Britain. The colonists no more owed political allegiance to the inhabitants of England than these did to the remaining inhabitants of the original homes of the Angles and Saxons. The assistance which the British Parliament had given them against foreign enemies was no reason for its claiming political authority; any debt in this respect could amply be met by the grant of commercial privileges. Like John Adams and James Wilson, Jefferson held that the existing link between the American colonies and Britain was a contractual not a prescriptive one.

"That settlement having been thus effected in the wilds of America, the emigrants thought proper to adopt that system of laws, under which they had hitherto lived in the mother country, and to continue their union with her, by submitting themselves to the same common sovereign, who was thereby made the central link, connecting the several parts of the empire thus newly multiplied."

In other words, the communities composing the Empire were equal in status, and linked solely by their allegiance to a common Crown. One hundred and fifty years before, Lord Balfour framed for the Imperial Conference of 1926 the famous definition of the status of the self-governing Dominions of the British Commonwealth, subsequently embodied in the Statute of Westminster, Jefferson had laid down precisely the same principle. It is an interesting example of the permanent character of the major problems of politics and of the relatively narrow margins within which their solutions can be found.

From this point of view it was possible to regard the Acts of the British Parliament of which the Americans complained as "acts of power, assumed by a body of men foreign to their constitutions," and the King is entreated to recommend their revocation in his capacity as "yet the only mediatory power between the several States of the British Empire." The King possesses, admits Jefferson, "the executive powers of the laws in every State; but they are the laws of the particular State, which he is to administer within that State, and not those of any one within the limits of another."

The freedom of language which the Americans use is becoming to a "free people claiming their rights as derived from the laws of nature, and not as the gift of their Chief Magistrate." "Kings," declares Jefferson, "are the servants not the proprietors of the people." George III will have to think and act for himself on American affairs, since he has no American ministers, but this should not be difficult, since "the whole art of government consists in being honest." This is the important post in which fortune has placed him "holding the balance of a great, if well-poised empire"; just dealing will

57

"establish fraternal love and harmony through the whole empire."

The *Summary View* is worth considering in this detail, because it illustrates very clearly both Jefferson's conception of the Empire and the dominant place taken in his thinking by the theory of natural rights. The specific grievances of which Jefferson complains are those which might have been expected from the history of the past decade. Typical of Jefferson himself was the emphasis laid upon the veto of colonial acts for ending the African slave trade. This had shown that the King preferred "the immediate advantages of a few British corsairs to the lasting interests of the American States, and to the rights of human nature, deeply wounded by this infamous practice." It was nature also which was the foundation of their other claims. Thus the American colonists, according to Jefferson, possessed "the exercise of a free trade with all parts of the world . . . as of natural right." And when dealing with the suspension of the New York legislature, he declares that "not only the principles of common sense, but the common feelings of human nature must be surrendered up, before his Majesty's subjects here can be persuaded to believe that they hold their political existence at the will of a British Parliament."

Jefferson was not among those nominated to the first Continental Congress which met at Philadelphia on September 5, 1774 and remained in session until October 26. The weight of opinion there was still strongly in favour of seeking redress for American grievances within the empire, and the main upshot of the Congress's deliberations was the establishment of machinery for tightening the boycott of British trade, which was relied upon for forcing the imperial Government to accept the American claims. Jefferson seems to have been disappointed that the Congress had not gone farther, and particularly that the several colonies were only to be bound by those decisions to which their own delegates had assented.

On the other hand, even in his absence, the Congress had gone a long way towards accepting the point of view with which he had identified himself. It had rejected Joseph Galloway's plan for a new imperial constitution within which the American colonies would form a subordinate union, and the Declaration of Rights, adopted on October 14, had placed "the immutable laws of nature" in the forefront of the sources from which the colonies derived their rights.

The main feature of the new Association embodying the non-intercourse decision was the establishment of committees for its enforcement in every county, city or town. Jefferson himself was placed at the head of the poll for the Committee of Safety of Albemarle County, and was also elected to represent the county at the second Virginia Convention on March 20, 1775. On this occasion the division between the moderate and the radical elements again showed itself. The central point at issue was a proposal by Patrick Henry for establishing and arming a militia for the "protection and defence of the country." This meant, as Henry admitted, that hope of reconciliation must be abandoned, and that there was no way out but an appeal to arms. Jefferson was among those who supported the proposal, which was eventually carried by the narrow margin of 65 votes to 60, and he was appointed to the committee formed to carry out the scheme.

Meanwhile, events in the colony were moving to a crisis. In the previous autumn the Governor, Lord Dunmore, had espoused the cause of the Virginia expansionists to the extent of leading a war against the Shawnee Indians in Kentucky, but this had won him scant popularity on the tide-water. New land regulations promulgated by the Crown forbade the settlement of unsurveyed lands, and raised the purchase price and the quit-rents for such areas as were opened for settlement. In fact, the land policy now finally formulated meant a virtual embargo on western expansion. Most Virginians were indifferent to this issue, and the Quebec Act of June 1774, extending the southern boundaries of Canada so as to include territories in which the Virginian land speculators had claims, seems to have been attacked, not on this score, but because of the religious and political implications of the growth of a Catholic and non-self-governing colony.

The Convention of March 1775, in which expansionist elements were prominent, thanked Dunmore for his Indian War but denounced the new land policy, and denied the Crown the right to raise rents in terms reminiscent of the *Summary View*. Relations with the Governor grew still more tense after Dunmore issued a proclamation stating that he intended to prevent Virginia from sending deputies to a second Continental Congress which had been called for May. The removal in April of a store of gunpowder from the Williamsburg magazine to a British warship, the *Fowey*, and the news of the colonists' clash with British troops at Lexington in Massachusetts, brought matters to a head. Dunmore, in a last attempt at conciliation, called a meeting of the Assembly for June 1. A week later he retired on board the *Fowey*, and British rule in Virginia was virtually at an end.

Jefferson had been appointed by the Assembly to the committee set up to consider the proposals for conciliation advanced by the British Prime Minister, Lord North, and he was the author of the report which it presented to the House on June 12. The report rejected Lord North's proposals, since they implied a right on the part of Parliament to "intermeddle with the support of the civil government of the colonies," did not undo the measures taken against Massachusetts, and did not free Americans to trade with the rest of the world. Most important of all was the stress laid upon the fact that the matter was now one for all the colonies; Virginians could not in honour act alone, without being "base deserters of that union" to which they had acceded. Although the resolution ended by expressing the hope that Americans might yet see "reunited, the blessing of liberty and property, and the most permanent harmony with Great Britain," the birth of a separate American nation was now very close at hand.

On June 20, 1775, Jefferson arrived at Philadelphia to take part in the second Continental Congress. The deliberations of this body had already begun. The repercussions of events in New England were now making themselves felt throughout the colonies, and everywhere the extra-legal power of the committees was taking shape and a military organization being improvised. The political coalition of the radicals of Massachusetts and Virginia which was the basis for the Congress's work was being forged largely through the patient diplomacy of John Adams. Its first fruit was the appointment of George Washington as commander-in-chief of all the continental forces. Jefferson's first assignment was to draw up a proclamation for Washington to issue upon taking up his command. In the end, however, the "Declaration on Taking Arms" was mainly written by the more conservative John Dickinson, and Jefferson's share was confined to the last four and a half paragraphs.

It was Dickinson too, who prepared the petition to the King, signed on July 8, which represented the surviving hopes of the moderates. But Jefferson was entrusted with preparing the text of Congress's reply to Lord North's proposals, and this document followed closely that which he had drafted for the Virginia Assembly.

August 1775 saw Jefferson once more in Virginia, but late in September he left once more for Philadelphia, where the Congress was deeply involved in the heavy task of building an army. It was at about this time that Jefferson appears to have abandoned his earlier point of view that the matter at issue was one solely between Parliament and the colonies, and that reconciliation was still possible on the basis of a common allegiance to the Crown. For, on November 29, in a letter to his relative John

Randolph—one of those who, despairing of reconciliation, had preferred to seek refuge in England
rather than countenance rebellion—Jefferson for
the first time directly attacked George III, as the
"bitterest enemy" the Americans had. "We want,"
he declared, "neither inducement nor power to declare and assert a separation. It is will alone which
is wanting, and that is growing apace under the
fostering hand of our King."

The immediate cause of this change of viewpoint
was presumably the news of the King's intransigent
speech at the opening of Parliament on October 26.
In January 1776, Tom Paine's *Common Sense* crystallized the growing feeling for independence, and
in its straightforward exposition of an egalitarian
democratic viewpoint, provided a weapon of propaganda more powerful than anything so far produced by native American writers.

By this date, however, Jefferson was on his way
home again, and for the next four months domestic
affairs and ill health detained him at Monticello,
where his position as commander-in-chief of the
county militia kept him busy enough. During these
months, the movement for independence gathered
speed, the first steps in that sense being taken in
the Carolinas. In May 1776, a new Virginia Convention met, and on the 15th instructed its delegates to
Congress to propose that the colonies declare their
independence, enter into a confederation, and con-
clude any desirable foreign alliances. The power of
forming governments for the internal concerns of
the separate colonies was to be left to their own
legislatures.

Jefferson, although elected a member of this body, had not wished to delay longer his return to Philadelphia, where he took his seat again on May 14. On the following day, May 15, Congress passed a resolution recommending that the separate colonies establish for themselves the new forms of government of their choice. On June 7, Richard Henry Lee introduced and John Adams seconded the two vital resolutions, the first declaring the "United Colonies" were, and of right ought to be, "free and independent States," and the second suggesting the preparation of a plan of confederation for their approval. The moment was a crucial one. The invasion of Canada in the previous autumn had failed to coerce that colony into joining with the Americans; now the news came that a commission sent to seek the same end by peaceful means had been rebuffed. Preparations for British military action on a larger scale were reported from Canada and elsewhere. The best hope of the Americans seemed to lie in obtaining the aid of Britain's rivals, France and Spain. Those who advocated a declaration of independence did so largely on the ground that no satisfactory negotiations with foreign countries were possible unless the Americans could offer the guarantees and commercial advantages which only an independent nation could provide. But the conservative members from the Middle Colonies were unconvinced, and succeeded in having the main question postponed until July 1. On June 11, a committee was appointed for preparing a declaration of independence should such a step eventually be agreed upon. The committee's members were

Thomas Jefferson, John Adams, Benjamin Franklin, Roger Sherman and Robert R. Livingston. By the end of the month, evidence was rapidly accumulating that the less forward colonies were coming into line. On July 1, consideration of the question of independence was duly resumed, and the issue was debated for the next two days. On July 2, without a negative voice, but with New York abstaining, the resolution for Independence was passed. It now remained for this to be set forth in the manner best calculated to win the approval of the people and the sympathies of the rest of the world.

Few historical documents have received more careful study than the Declaration of Independence, and its evolution is fully examined in Carl Becker's book, the *Declaration of Independence*, and in the more recent publication of facsimiles of the various drafts edited by Julian P. Boyd. Nevertheless, the accounts of Jefferson and Adams given at various dates some time after the events have not been reconciled; nor do we know the reason why the drafting was entrusted to Jefferson, rather than to the Massachusetts statesman who had done so much for the cause of independence. It is certain that the draft of June 28 was Jefferson's work, although amended in consultation with Adams and Franklin.

The debate on the draft Declaration began on July 2, and was continued throughout the two subsequent days. Jefferson himself took no part in the debate, leaving it to Adams to defend the draft, which he did ably and pertinaciously against attacks from many quarters. A good many changes were made, both verbal and substantive. Jefferson's

65

own contemporary notes give his version of the reasons for the most important of these:

"The pusillanimous idea that we had friends in England worth keeping terms with, still haunted the minds of many. For this reason those passages which conveyed censures on the people of England were struck out, lest they should give them offense. The clause too, reprobating the enslaving the inhabitants of Africa, was struck out in complaisance to South Carolina and Georgia, who had never attempted to restrain the importation of slaves, and who on the contrary still wished to continue it. Our Northern brethren also I believe felt a little tender under those censures; for tho' their people have very few slaves themselves, yet they had been pretty considerable carriers of them to others."

Of the verbal changes, the most interesting is that Jefferson's original reference to "inherent and inalienable rights" was altered to "certain unalienable rights." Congress also struck out Jefferson's reference to the Colonies' voluntary adoption of one common King at the time their Governments were formed. And it was Congress which inserted in the final sentence the reference to "the protection of divine providence." Since in Jefferson's own first draft the words "from their equal creation" stand in place of the "endowed by their creator" of the Declaration as submitted to Congress, we may infer that had Jefferson alone been responsible from start to finish for the framing and phrasing of the document, the only reference to the Deity would have been the one to "Nature's God."

It is clear that by 1776 Jefferson was emancipated

from the religious orthodoxy of his upbringing, and was, if a deist rather than the atheist which his political enemies were later to see in him, disposed in the political as in the moral field to seek a sanction for his beliefs in the unaided operations of the human reason alone. An undogmatic deism of this kind was indeed characteristic of several of the leading figures of Jefferson's own generation, although few were to combine it with so strong an anti-clerical bias. But deism of this kind was too aristocratic a creed to survive in a more democratic age, and Jefferson's party in later days found the bulk of its adherents among classes for whom a modicum of religious observance was a necessary guarantee of right feeling.

Even when Congress had done with it, the Declaration of Independence was a thoroughly Jeffersonian document; it bears a strong resemblance to his *Summary View* written two years earlier. Once again the form is a simple one: the statement of a political philosophy, its application to the American colonies, an enumeration of the steps by which their rights had been invaded and, as a conclusion, the announcement of the dissolution of the political connection between the American States and Great Britain.

It is the opening paragraphs which alone concern the student of American democracy, for the usurpations of George III had passed into history. These opening paragraphs, whose effect, in stamping upon the mind of the American nation the doctrine of natural rights, has been of the profoundest significance, finally ran as follows:

"When in the Course of human events, it becomes necessary for one people to dissolve the political bands, which have connected them with another, and to assume among the powers of the earth, the separate and equal station to which the Laws of Nature and of Nature's God entitle them, a decent respect to the opinions of mankind requires that they should declare the causes which impel them to the separation. We hold these truths to be self-evident, that all men are created equal, that they are endowed by their Creator with certain unalienable Rights, that among these are Life, Liberty and the pursuit of Happiness. That to secure these rights, Governments are instituted among Men, deriving their just powers from the consent of the governed. That whenever any form of Government becomes destructive of these ends, it is the Right of the People to alter or to abolish it, and to institute new Government, laying its foundation on such principles and organizing its powers in such form, as to them shall seem most likely to effect their Safety and Happiness. Prudence, indeed, will dictate that Governments long established should not be changed for light and transient causes; and accordingly all experience hath shown, that mankind are more disposed to suffer while evils are sufferable, than to right themselves by abolishing the forms to which they are accustomed. But when a long train of abuses and usurpations, pursuing invariably the same Object evinces a design to reduce them under absolute Despotism, it is their right, it is their duty to throw off such Government, and to provide new Guards for their future security."

The reader of the Declaration of Independence must even now be on his guard against the compelling qualities of Jefferson's literary style. The truths which he calls self-evident were not self-evident at all either to his contemporaries or to later generations. The notion that all men are born equal was not accepted either in theory or in practice then or later. For "all men" is a description which (as Loyalists pointed out) knows nothing of distinctions of race and colour. The replacement in the familiar formula, life, liberty and *property*, of the last of these, by the *pursuit of happiness*, was a challenge to much of the implicit as well as the explicit philosophy upon which human societies had hitherto been built. The Declaration of Independence was a revolutionary document; it still is.

Jefferson, in a letter written towards the close of his life (to Henry Lee, May 8, 1825), said that his object in writing the Declaration had been "not to find out new principles, or new arguments, never before thought of, not merely to say things which had never been said before; but to place before mankind the common sense of the subject in terms so plain and firm as to command their assent . . . neither aiming at originality of principle or sentiment, nor yet copied from any particular and previous writing, it was intended to be an expression of the American mind."

In a sense this was true, and the Declaration of Independence would not otherwise have had the effect which it did. European philosophers, for all their eighteenth-century preoccupation with happiness, had never contemplated happiness as a right

—it was too far removed from the circumstances of the old world. But in the new world, even the "pursuit of happiness" was not original, although never previously enshrined with such conviction in a formal state paper. The idea itself figured in a pamphlet written in 1770 and published in 1774, by James Wilson, the Pennsylvanian statesman, with which Jefferson is known to have been acquainted. And the Virginia Bill of Rights, drawn up by George Mason, and adopted by the Virginia Assembly on May 12, 1776—a document which the Virginian delegates at Philadelphia must have known—included, among the inherent rights of men, the "pursuing and obtaining happiness and safety." Nevertheless, it was essentially Jefferson who, in the words of Gilbert Chinard, "gave currency to an expression which was to influence deeply and even to mold American life." The originality lay in Jefferson's ability at the crucial moment to find language in which these floating elements in the American consciousness could be crystallized into a permanent form and so transmitted to posterity.

It was, finally, not America alone which was to be influenced by the Declaration, although only an American could have written it. For the fact of American independence gave force to the theory by which it was defended: "The accomplished fact," as Carl Becker wrote, "conferred upon the Declaration a distinction, a fame which could not be ignored, and gave to its philosophy of human rights the support of a concrete historical example."

Chapter Four
Virginian Statesman
(1776–1784)

THE Declaration of Independence marked the beginning rather than the end of the work of the Continental Congress. A permanent form of union had to be established, the organization of national defence perpetuated and strengthened, and negotiations carried on with foreign Powers. It might have been anticipated that Jefferson, whose reputation was now established and who had been elected to many of the most important committees, would play a prominent part in the work to come. But although re-elected a delegate that summer, he declined to serve, and on September 2, having attended the early debates on the Articles of Confederation, he left Philadelphia for home. Later that month he was nominated by Congress as one of the Commissioners to be sent to treat with the French, but again refused to leave Virginia.

It is clear that the motives which led Jefferson to leave the national scene were largely personal and domestic: the increasingly precarious health of his wife made him unwilling to be separated from her by the long journey from Monticello to Philadelphia. But it should not be assumed that he regarded his withdrawal as indicating the end of his participation in active politics. Throughout his life,

Jefferson regarded his work in Virginia as at least as important as that which he performed as a national statesman. Indeed, his political philosophy, with its emphasis on the value of small units, his conviction that what mattered was a healthy society rather than a strong Government, his preference for the imaginative and philosophical sides of legislative work over the day-to-day burdens of administration and diplomacy, the fact that Jefferson, for all his shrewdness, had the weaknesses as well as the strength of the intellectual—all these made the Assembly of his own state rather than Congress the natural scene for his activity. And it was in the Virginia legislature, at Williamsburg, that he once more took his seat on October 11, 1776.

The remoulding of Virginia's institutions was no easy task. For Jefferson, the achievement of republican government was only a step towards the establishment of a genuinely republican society. The removal of the royal governor and his council and of the imperial veto were of little use if the laws remained such as to favour the accumulation of property in a few hands and to confirm the owners of that property in the seats of political power. Freedom was only a word if the intellectual life of the state was to remain under the domination of an established church, and the enjoyment of both political and religious freedom could only be sustained in the long run by the establishment of a system of popular education designed to fit the people for their republican institutions. On the other hand, there were powerful elements in the colony for whom the breach with the mother-country was intended to be the last step, not the first step, in the Revolution.

The clash of parties had already shown itself in the matter of framing a constitution for the state. It was on May 15, 1776, that Congress had recommended that the states take measures to substitute new forms of government for the old machinery of colonial rule. On the following day, Jefferson wrote in confidence to Thomas Nelson, a friend of his in the Virginia Convention, suggesting that if that body proposed to go ahead with framing a Constitution, it might be advisable to recall their delegates at Philadelphia, since it would be "a work of the most interesting nature and such as every individual would wish to have his voice in." His anxiety as to what might be done in his absence was reflected in his remarking: "In truth, it is the whole object of the present controversy; for should a bad government be instituted for us in future, it had been as well to have accepted at first the bad one offered to us from beyond the water without the risk and expence of contest."

But the Virginia Convention was not disposed to consider the presence of any single person indispensable, and on May 15, the day on which they had instructed their delegates to press for independence, the members also appointed a committee to frame a plan of government and a Bill of Rights. Jefferson was not prepared to allow his views to go unknown, and on receiving word of the Convention's decision, set himself to prepare a draft Bill which could be used as the basis of a Constitution. When his friend George Wythe left Philadelphia for Williamsburg in the middle of June, the document was ready for him.

Jefferson's plan went a long way in the direction of democracy. The suffrage was to be granted to all having a freehold estate of a quarter of an acre in the towns or twenty-five acres in the country, and to all persons who had paid "scot and lot" for two years. The representation of counties and boroughs was to be proportionate to their population. Purchases of lands from the Indians were to be made by the legislature, and lands so purchased were to be allotted without payment in lots limited to fifty acres per head. The lands claimed by Virginia in the west were eventually to be formed into free and separate states. Other proposals gave expression to Jefferson's views in favour of the equal partition of inheritances, religious toleration and disestablishment, the freedom of the Press and the prohibition of the further importation of slaves.

By the time that the Convention received this document, its own plans were far advanced. The alignment of political parties in Virginia had been changed by the events of the preceding months. The more conservative elements had wished Virginia to go on alone with the establishment of her independence and the framing of her institutions. The radical element, headed by the Lees, had advocated independence by Congressional action and the framing by Congress of a uniform plan for the government of the states. In this way they hoped that the more radical New Englanders would be able to influence affairs in Virginia. But as far as constitution-making was concerned, they had accepted the comparatively conservative document framed by George Mason; and of Jefferson's draft, only the preamble was made use of, and set in front of Mason's work.

Much of what Jefferson wanted was, however, obtainable as ordinary legislation, and when he took his seat in the new legislature, it was with a view to putting through a definite programme of reforms. In this he had the support of such men as Wythe, Mason and James Madison, against the strenuous opposition of such leaders of the old order as Edmund Pendleton and Robert Carter Nicholas.

For a society so overwhelmingly agrarian as that of Virginia, the most important laws were those dealing with the inheritance of land. Hitherto, the practice in Virginia had been that of the English common law. Primogeniture was observed, and the device of entail made it impossible for estates to be divided or sold. As Jefferson's biographer, Henry Randall, put it, writing in the nineteenth-century heyday of democratic exaltation:

"In all the lower counties of the state, a large portion of the lands were divided into great estates, held from generation to generation by the older sons, in the same way, and producing the same political and social consequences, that are now witnessed from the like causes, in England and some other European countries. The political and social framework was essentially aristocratic, producing the luxury, æsthetic culture, showy and apparently prosperous appearances incidental to such a condition, and which are often mistaken by superficial observers for the highest and best national development. But the few controlled the many in politics, lorded it over them in society, monopolized what was equally theirs by natural right, and finally by holding more than they could put to its best uses, diminished the aggregate resources of the state."

In a month of sternly fought debate against vehement and skilled opposition, Jefferson succeeded in getting through both Houses of the legislature a Bill for the abolition of entails, and a major blow was struck at the foundations of an order of society of which he himself was the outstanding product.

At the same time, Jefferson obtained agreement to the appointment of a committee to revise the entire legal code of Virginia, and a Bill for this purpose was passed on October 24, 1776. Pendleton, who was one of the five members appointed, proposed that they should draw up an entirely new code, but this was rejected by Jefferson on the ground that a new code would give endless opportunities for litigation until the Courts had established a body of agreed interpretations. He had no intention of magnifying the power of the judiciary. Agreement was reached on a revision of the existing body of common law and of the English and colonial statutes. The actual work was divided between Jefferson, Wythe and Pendleton; to Jefferson's share fell the common law and English statute law prior to the establishment of the colony—a testimony to his reputation for legal and historical scholarship.

The work of revision took until early in 1779,

and in June of that year the result was reported to the legislature in the form of 126 separate Bills. These incorporated many important changes of substance. The law of descent finally abolished primogeniture, and subjected real estate to the same laws as personal property, inheritable in equal proportions by the next of kin.

The new criminal code for which Jefferson was largely responsible was inspired by the doctrines of Beccaria, and marked a considerable humanitarian advance, particularly in the limitation of the death penalty to cases of treason and murder, although the incorporation of the principle of retaliation disfigures it to the modern eye. It proved too advanced at its first presentation, and in spite of Madison's efforts, it was not until 1796 that the Virginian criminal laws were revised along the lines of Jefferson's proposals.

The severest struggle was that over religion. The growing body of dissenters had looked to the severance of the British connection to end the monopoly of the (Anglican) episcopalian church. With this demand, Jefferson had full personal and political sympathies. In a severe struggle in the legislature between October and December 1776, Jefferson was so far successful as to secure the abolition of all laws making criminal the practice or failure to practise any religious creed, to exempt dissenters from the payment of tithes, and to suspend temporarily their levy even from members of the establishment. On the other hand, if, as is probable, the majority of the colony were by now dissenters, the legislature was still predominently episcopalian and wished to make some provision for the established church.

On June 13, 1779, Jefferson's Bill for the Establishment of Religious Freedom was introduced. This Bill declared religious freedom to be a natural right of mankind, forbade any discrimination between people in their civil capacities on account of their religious beliefs, and left the support of religious institutions entirely to the voluntary action of their adherents. The opposition to so far-reaching a step was very great, and the most that could be obtained was the final abolition of levies for the support of the church. The supporters of the Establishment were still strong, and in 1784, with the support of many of the dissenters, they introduced a new compulsory tax, but with the proviso that each person could choose to which denomination his contribution should be allotted. Jefferson was then away in Europe, but the struggle over the proposal involved on different sides most of the other notable men in the state. For the proposed tax stood George Washington, Patrick Henry and R. H. Lee; against them were George Mason, James Madison and George Nicholas. Eventually Madison succeeded in getting up so great an agitation that the proposal was dropped, and in 1786 Jefferson's Bill, in a slightly amended form, at last became law.

As important as religious freedom, and for Jefferson as indissolubly linked with political liberty, was the education of the people at large. For this purpose, he framed three Bills as part of the revised code: a Bill for the more general diffusion of knowledge; a Bill for amending the constitution of his own college, William and Mary, so as to remove its theological bias and modernize the curriculum; and a Bill for the establishment of a public library.

Of these three Bills, the first was the most remarkable, since it proposed a complete system of free tax-supported elementary schools for all boys and girls other than slaves, a further tier of grammar schools to which boys from the elementary schools should be eligible through a system of scholarships, and finally scholarships for the most promising of these pupils to enable them to attend the college.

An examination of the language of the Bill as well as of its provisions shows that it was far from being an expression of the modern attitude that education is a right to which each child is entitled according to the full extent of his natural endowments. It was not mass education but selective education with which Jefferson was concerned. Society for its own sake could not afford not to train such children of poor parents as showed genuine promise. The impulse was civic and political, not egalitarian.

The Jeffersonian doctrine, that the best way of guarding against tyranny is to "illuminate, as far as practicable, the minds of the people at large, and more especially to give them knowledge of those facts which history exhibiteth," is set out in full in section one of the Bill itself. Whence, he writes:

"It becomes expedient for promoting the publick happiness that those persons, whom nature hath endowed with genius and virtue, should be rendered by liberal education worthy to receive and able to guard the sacred deposit of the rights and liberties of their fellow citizens, and that they should be called to that charge without regard to wealth, birth or other accidental condition or circumstance; but the indigence of the greater number disabling them from so educating at their own expence, those of their children whom nature hath fitly formed and disposed to become useful instruments for the public, it is better that such should be sought for and educated at the common expence of all, than that the happiness of all should be confined [?confided] to the weak and wicked."

In his edition of the correspondence between Jefferson and the French thinker of the physiocratic school Pierre-Samuel du Pont de Nemours, the founder of the industrial dynasty of that name, Professor Chinard pointed out that similar views had been expressed in France, in the *Mémoires sur les Municipalités* (1775), which, though signed by Turgot, were almost wholly the work of Du Pont. But Jefferson's ideas were worked out independently, and it was their circulation during Jefferson's stay in Paris which, Chinard suggests, gave the impetus to French action along these lines. The essentials of his Bill were to be found in the proposals submitted to the French legislatures between 1791 and 1796. And the French educational system, with its pyramid of institutions and ladder of scholarships, as fully developed under the Third Republic, may thus claim a Jeffersonian ancestry.

But if Jefferson was to find the French receptive to his bold ideas on education, his fellow-Virginians were less so. The scheme was too costly to commend itself to the people who would have to pay for it.

When an Elementary Education Bill was passed in 1796, the counties were allowed to opt whether or not to operate it, and it would seem that not a single one did so. The other two Bills were not adopted. Jefferson's hopes of Virginia taking a lead in the educational field were never fulfilled and it was left for others to set the pace.

Even more characteristic of the lack of harmony between Jefferson's far-sighted and imaginative perception of social questions and the prejudices of his fellow-citizens, was his failure to get them to use the occasion of revising the laws to tackle the root problem of negro slavery. His own idea was that all slaves born after a certain date should be emancipated, and that the freed negroes should be deported and colonized outside the bounds of the United States, but he found insufficient support to warrant him in bringing it forward.

This account of Jefferson's legislative activity omits such questions as fell to the Assembly to decide in connection with the war; for example, the payments of debts owing to British subjects—a matter upon which Jefferson took a generous view. Indeed, his attitude, and later that of Madison, Mason and the Lees, effectively dispose of the suggestion that the Virginia planters joined the revolutionary movement in order to free themselves from their debts to British merchants. The final repudiation was due to Patrick Henry and his radical yeoman following.

Jefferson's biographers have tended to consider his period of domestic leadership in Virginia as one whose high democratic purposes command unstinted applause. "It took," says S. K. Padover, "nine years of struggle to transform Virginia into a democratic commonwealth. . . . It was a bloodless revolution, carefully planned and calmly executed by the young philosopher-planter who had a vision of free men in a free land." But it may be hazarded that the Virginia of Jefferson's later years and of the decades which followed his death was far from being the democratic commonwealth of his vision, and that such changes as there were owed most to the rapid exhaustion of the soil and the consequent impoverishment of the planter-class. Nor indeed would Jefferson have applauded a transfer of power without a corresponding spread of enlightenment. Of the first five Presidents of the United States, four were Virginians, but after Monroe, the last in the line of the Jeffersonian succession, the influence of the state in national affairs declined steeply.

One may well refer to the summary of Jefferson's work for Virginia contained in the history of his Presidency written by his predecessor's gifted great-grandson. In Henry Adams's view, the belief of Jefferson and Madison, that the freedom of religion which had worked so well in Pennsylvania would work in Virginia was wrong. No sooner was the support of the state removed than the church perished, and the result was not all gain, since Jefferson failed to persuade his fellow-citizens of the virtues of an alternative culture based on secular education. "Jefferson's reforms," wrote Adams, "crippled and impoverished the gentry, but did little for the people, and for the slaves nothing."

The question of Virginia's future was of course

inseparable from that of the disposition of the western lands, and Jefferson's attitude towards this problem has not been altogether satisfactorily explained. Jefferson's connections with western expansionism date back to the very beginning of his career, since he inherited his father's share in the claims of the Loyal Company, founded in 1749. Still more significant, in all probability, was the fact that Dr. Thomas Walker, one of his guardians, was the most important figure in the whole history of the land-speculating interests in Virginia between the French and Indian War and the end of the Revolution.

It would almost certainly be an error to think of Jefferson's interest in the western lands as being due to the desire for personal gain. His whole social philosophy hinged on the idea of an ever-open frontier, and his attitude towards the question was consequently a more political one and a more consistent one than that of the other planter-magnates, nearly all of whom had some kind of personal interest in one or more land companies. As we have seen, one of the features of his proposed constitution for Virginia was the provision for the parcellation of unsettled lands in small units. The Revolutionary war by no means diminished the movement of settlers westward, especially into Kentucky, and the agents of the different land companies were active in trying to secure the diversion of forces from the main field of conflict to the interior, where the Indians might be thrown back and new areas opened up. It was these conflicting interests which explain the long delay in the ratification of the

Articles of Confederation, the first formal constitution of the United States, since those States which had no western land claims wished the possession of all western lands to be vested in Congress. This obstacle was not overcome until 1781.

Jefferson, like his friends in the Adams-Lee group, did not approve of the expedition sent out by Congress from Pittsburgh in the autumn of 1778. But together with Mason and Wythe, he supported Patrick Henry—himself rather ambiguously involved in a variety of land-speculations—in sending out the simultaneous expedition of George Rogers Clark, acting under Virginia's own authority. This force captured the British posts at Kaskaskia and Vincennes, in the old north-west between the Ohio and the Missouri.

The Virginian radicals, whose victory in the state's affairs was signalized by Jefferson's election to the governorship in June 1779, were expansionist in temper, although without strong sympathies for the frontiersmen. Jefferson, as governor, continued Patrick Henry's policy, and in the autumn of 1779 a post was established at the mouth of the Ohio and named Fort Jefferson. More important, however, was the final enactment of legislation for settling the land question in the western areas of the state itself. Although the law of June 22, 1779, setting up a land-office, was introduced by George Mason, there seems to be no doubt but that Jefferson had a hand in its framing. But whatever his intentions, the result was not by any means to facilitate the increase in the number of small proprietors envisaged in his scheme of three years earlier. In the words of an authority upon the question, Professor T. P. Abernethy:

"The land office act of 1779 was a colossal mistake. . . . There is an element of historical irony in the fact that Jefferson, the father of democracy, should have helped to draft the act, by which democracy was defeated in Virginia at the moment when it might have had its birth. The result was that within a few years, Robert Morris came to own over one and a half million acres and Alexander Walcott a million acres of Virginia's western lands, and most of that remaining fell into the hands of other absentee speculators, who paid in depreciated currency, a price equivalent in some cases to about fifty cents the hundred acres. Thus the growth of the country was retarded, the resident population forced to protect the property of those who took no part in its defense, and the great public domain was exploited by a few individuals for their private gain."

There is no period of Jefferson's career which has laid him open to more abuse than that of his tenure of the office of Governor of Virginia. It is difficult to think of anyone making a success of the office at that particular time in the state's history unless possessed of exceptional executive and military qualities. Jefferson was no Washington.

The general situation of the United States was critical. Throughout the war, enthusiasm for the cause was lukewarm in many areas, and few states were willing to supply the men and materials for the fighting outside their own borders that was necessary if the war was to be waged and won as a whole. The seizure of Boston in the spring of 1776 was offset by Washington's defeats in New York later in the year. In 1777 the major British effort to cut the colonies in two, by driving down from Canada to link up with the forces in New York, was foiled by Burgoyne's defeat and surrender at Saratoga. But Philadelphia fell after Washington's defeat at Germantown, and the under-equipped continental army faced the hardships of a cruel winter at Valley Forge.

The victory at Saratoga was decisive enough to bring about a major political triumph for the new Republic, since an alliance with France was concluded on February 6, 1778. This made it possible to reject the conciliatory proposals offered by Lord North at this juncture—proposals which, if fully implemented, would have reformed the empire along lines very similar to those advocated by Jefferson in the *Summary View*. Nevertheless, although France joined in the war at once, and Spain in June 1779, the advantages from this were slow in accruing. By the winter of 1778–9 Washington's spirits were at their lowest. Congress was failing altogether to secure from the states the financial aid which it required, and had no power to secure itself. It was forced to rely, for maintaining its armies, upon rapidly depreciating paper money. The French alliance also introduced new complications into the question of the ultimate American war aims—a question upon which, particularly as it regarded the future boundaries of the United States, Congress itself was deeply divided.

With the failure of the plan to make Canada the

main base of operations, the British turned the weight of the war southwards. Their plan was to seize Georgia and to work northwards. In 1778 they took Savannah, and in 1779 advanced into the interior of Georgia and South Carolina. In the month preceding Jefferson's election to the governorship, the British made their first big seaborne raid on Virginia and caused considerable destruction. Jefferson found the state's treasury as empty as that of Congress, and Washington insisted that its resources be devoted to the support of the main armies operating in the Middle States and in the Carolinas, instead of being held back for local defence.

Jefferson's correspondence with Washington shows him struggling hard to fulfil Virginia's obligations to the common cause, despite the ravages of the British, and of their privateers at sea, and despite the Indian menace on the frontier. There were the administrative difficulties resulting from the lack of communications between the new state capital, Richmond, and the other states, and those caused by the lack of wheeled transport in a country normally wholly dependent on water-transport. Neither in men, money, nor supplies did Virginia come up to the demands of its Governor and of Congress.

In 1780 further disasters befell the American cause. Charleston was captured in May and the whole of South Carolina overrun. In the last days of the year a British fleet arrived in Chesapeake Bay. Richmond was occupied on January 5, 1781, and Jefferson had to make a hurried move in order to avoid capture. Although the British occupation only lasted for a couple of days, the affair was an unfortunate one, and was heavily exploited by Jefferson's political rivals. In the spring, with Washington still intent on the conquest of New York, Virginia was submitted to the ordeal of a full-scale invasion. Some federal reinforcements were sent under Lafayette, whom Jefferson now met for the first time. But Jefferson was again forced to abandon Richmond and to retire to Charlottesville, which became the seat of government. In June a British raiding party got as far as Charlottesville itself, and only narrowly missed seizing Jefferson in his own Monticello.

The meeting of the legislature on June 7, in its new retreat at Staunton, saw another outburst of criticism at Jefferson's expense. The opposition now revived a project which had been first suggested at the end of 1779—namely, to place full civil and military powers in the hands of a dictator. It was clearly intended, as on the previous occasion, that the dictator should be Patrick Henry, the popular hero of Virginian democracy. Not knowing that Jefferson had already determined not to seek re-election for the third year to which the Constitution entitled him, the opposition promoted a set of formal charges against Jefferson's conduct of affairs which it was hoped would get him out of the way. But the evidence that the project of a dictatorship would meet with general resistance caused it to be abandoned. Jefferson thereupon announced his withdrawal, and General Nelson was elected in his place and with his approval.

The military tide had now turned; in the south the British were pushed back on Charleston and Savannah; farther north Washington and the French admiral, de Grasse began the fortunate combination which forced the British commander Cornwallis on to the defensive, and led to his surrender at Yorktown on October 16, 1781. French aid by land and sea, and Washington's superior generalship, had proved decisive. Meanwhile, in September, Jefferson had accepted re-election to the Virginia legislature in order to answer the charges made against his conduct as governor. But the opposition made no move to press them, and on December 19 the Assembly formally exonerated Jefferson and expressed its full appreciation of his public services.

For Jefferson this was not enough. He was always very thin-skinned, and, lacking political ambition, had no intention of seeking or accepting the suffrages of those who had made him the target for criticisms which he felt to be totally unwarranted. He had already refused to return to Philadelphia as one of the state's delegates, and still earlier—in June—had rejected the offer of a place on the delegation of five to which Congress proposed to entrust the delicate negotiations in Europe made necessary by the approaching end of the war.

Once Jefferson had cleared his name, he wished to retire from public life like some ancient Roman, and live the life of a private citizen. Writing to Edmund Randolph on September 16th, he said: "I have taken my final leave of everything of that nature. I have retired to my farm, my family and books, from which I think nothing will ever separate me."

Jefferson's withdrawal from politics was also due to renewed anxieties about the health of his wife—all too well-founded, since she died on September 6, 1782, leaving two daughters aged ten and four, and a baby who survived only two years. Jefferson's own health, too, was for some time far from good. But neither the public nor the private reasons seemed adequate to his close collaborators such as Madison and James Monroe. Their verdict has been echoed by modern biographers. A man of thirty-eight, who has already proved himself in affairs of state, has not, it is argued, the right to quit it while further opportunities of service exist.

Jefferson's own long exculpation in a letter which he wrote to Monroe on May 20, 1782, has been dismissed as showing that wounded vanity was at the bottom of it all. And yet Jefferson was perfectly consistent in arguing that the state could require equal service from all its members but not perpetual service from anyone. "If we are made in some degree for others, yet in a greater are we made for ourselves. It were contrary to feeling and indeed ridiculous to suppose that a man had less right in himself than one of his neighbours or indeed all of them put together." "We are made for ourselves": that, after all, was fundamental to the idea of natural rights and hence to Jefferson's political creed. The management of one's own affairs, the bringing up of a family, the pursuit of intellectual interests—these were as worthy a way of spending one's time as any public business. No man is indispensable or should allow himself to think that he is. In this at least Jefferson was consistent throughout his life. Public life would be healthier if there were more of the same mind. Fully aware that power corrupts, Jefferson was never himself corrupted.

The critics of Jefferson's retirement have usually consoled themselves with the reflection that it was this leisure which gave him the opportunity for composing the most remarkable of his writings, the *Notes on Virginia*. These were drawn up in answer to a questionnaire about the conditions and resources of his state, sent to him in the spring of 1781 by M. Barbé de Marbois, the secretary of the French legation at Philadelphia. The work was composed in the same year and revised during the winter of 1782–3; it was first printed for private circulation in Paris soon after Jefferson's arrival there in the autumn of 1784. The appearance of a poor French translation in 1786 compelled Jefferson to assent to its publication in the original, and it appeared in the following year.

The *Notes* were thus not written for publication and were freer in their references to certain contentious subjects, such as slavery and the Virginian Constitution, than would have been likely in a published work. On the other hand, the form follows the order of the Frenchman's queries, and does not necessarily represent the way Jefferson would himself have chosen for presenting his native state and its problems to the world.

The *Notes on Virginia*, even when full account is taken of their circumstances, remain the major source of Jeffersonian doctrine and the best reflection of the many-sided intellect of the most "active-minded and sanguine of all Virginians" in Henry Adams's happy phrase. For its full appreciation, one would have to linger over the scientific side of the work, and such things as Jefferson's learned and witty refutation of the theory of Buffon and other European naturalists as to the degeneracy of the fauna of the New World.

But for the student of American democracy, the important passages are those in which Jefferson discloses his own social and political views. These passages have a particular interest, since the work was completed before his visit to Europe, and cannot be regarded as an effect of his direct contact with the intellectual world of pre-Revolutionary France.

It is obvious that by the time Jefferson wrote the *Notes on Virginia,* he was firmly convinced that a liberal democracy, in which the rights of individuals would have nothing to fear from the oppressions of government, and in which private and public morality would coincide, was an ideal only to be achieved in a society based upon a wide diffusion of landed property, and in which agrarian rather than mercantile or manufacturing interests would be dominant. Such had been the objective, if not the result, of the legislation he had inspired, and it now found its theoretical justification in a famous passage:

"Generally speaking, the proportion which the aggregate of the other classes of citizens bears in any state to that of its husbandmen, is the proportion of its unsound to its healthy parts, and is a good enough barometer whereby to measure its degree of corruption. While we have land to labour then, let us never wish to see our citizens occupied at a work-bench or twirling a distaff. Carpenters, masons, smiths, are wanting in husbandry; but, for the general operations of manufacture, let our workshops remain in Europe. It is better to carry provisions and materials to workmen there, than to bring them to the provisions and materials, and with them, their manners and principles. The loss by the transportation of commodities across the Atlantic will be made up in the happiness and permanence of government. The mobs of great cities add just so much to the support of pure government, as sores do to the strength of the human body. It is the manners and spirit of a people which preserve a republic in vigor. A degeneracy in these is a canker which soon eats to the heart of its laws and constitution."

A society of this kind was bound to be expansionist, and there seemed as yet no reason why expansion should not continue. Jefferson realized that the abundance of land led to wastefulness and low productivity, and that this ought to be remedied by encouraging the immigration of skilled foreign workers from whom new techniques could be acquired. But apart from this, Jefferson, with his insistence on the primacy of politics over economics, was sceptical of the current American belief in the virtues of rapid immigration.

"Civil government being the sole object of forming societies, its administration must be conducted by common consent. Every species of government has its specific principles. Ours perhaps are more peculiar than those of any other in the universe. It is a composition of the freest principles of the English constitution, with others derived from natural right and natural reason. To these nothing can be more opposed than the maxims of absolute monarchies. Yet from such we are to expect the greatest number of emigrants. They will bring with them the principles of the governments they leave, imbibed in their early youth; or, if able to throw them off, it will be in exchange for an unbounded licentiousness, passing, as is usual, from one extreme to another."

It will be seen that Jefferson made no concession to the principles by which were governed the country of his interlocutor. The same outspokenness is found in his defence of popular education as the only safeguard against the tyranny of rulers and the corruptions of democratic rule, and in his advocacy of complete toleration. Here he provocatively defied the embattled convictions of most respectable citizens: "The legitimate powers of government extend only to such acts as are injurious to others. But it does me no injury for my neighbor to say there are twenty gods, or no God. It neither picks my pocket nor breaks my leg." It was a remark not easily forgotten or forgiven.

Throughout the *Notes on Virginia* there runs a note of optimism. On one subject only does Jefferson reveal deep anxiety—"the unhappy influence on the manners of our people produced by the existence of slavery among us." He noted, above all, the disrespect into which human labour itself fell, where a class of slaves existed for its performance.

How could a democratic society permanently exist upon such a foundation? "Can the liberties of a nation be thought secure when we have removed their only firm basis, a conviction in the minds of the people that these liberties are of the gift of God? That they are not to be violated but with his wrath? Indeed I tremble for my country when I reflect that God is just; that his justice cannot sleep for ever."

But Jefferson, himself the owner of 150 slaves, while believing that the outcome must be total emancipation, either with the consent of the masters or against them, and possibly through their extirpation, did not flatter himself that the problem was an easy one. There was no prospect that the races could ever mingle, and the only hope was some scheme of colonization overseas such as he had in vain proposed at the time of the revision of the Virginia code and such as was to haunt humanitarian thought in America for more than one generation.

If slavery was the principal long-term threat to the democratic ideal which Jefferson cherished, the possibility of foreign war was the most important contingent menace. "Never was so much false arithmetic employed on any subject as that which has been employed to persuade nations that it is their interest to go to war." Rather than that occasions should arise of making war, Jefferson was prepared to see Americans abandon maritime commerce altogether and concentrate wholly upon agriculture. But this, he realized, was clearly outside the bounds of possibility. The Americans were already attached

95

to commerce and could not be dissuaded from it; therefore there would be wars, and the only thing to do was to make the best possible preparation for them. This preparation should be in the form of naval not land armaments. But there was, he argued, no need for a large navy such as would burden the country with as heavy a load of taxation as that which weighed upon European nations. For the strong naval powers of the Old World—Great Britain, France and Spain—were so placed that their colonial trade was vulnerable to attacks from the American mainland, while they would never, for fear of their rivals, be able to risk for its protection more than a small part of their fleets. What Jefferson had in mind was an American navy large enough to have nuisance value, and therefore one whose neutrality the Great Powers would be prepared to purchase, at the price of conceding to the Americans the right of free maritime commerce in time of war.

It would, then, be a mistake to regard Jefferson as a pacifist, although few great statesmen have been so eminently pacific in temperament. What he did believe in was a limited-liability theory of warfare; and circumstances were to give him ample opportunity of testing the efficacy of this theory.

The death of his wife removed one main reason for Jefferson's staying aloof from public affairs and provided an incentive for him to leave Monticello. In November 1782, he was asked to go to Europe to join in the peace negotiations; winter weather delayed his departure, and before he could sail, news reached the United States that a provisional treaty had been agreed to. He was therefore again available to serve his state, and the Virginia legislature once more nominated him as one of its delegates to Congress.

Jefferson resumed his seat in Congress in November 1783, and began at once a very active six months' work. His many duties included the chairmanship of the committee to consider the ratification of the peace treaty, and the drafting of the report on the coinage that led to the adoption of the dollar as the basic American monetary unit. He was in a position to acquire a very full picture of the major problems and resources of the United States at the moment when it was entering into its status as an acknowledged sovereign power.

The most significant of Jefferson's services was that which arose in connection with the final cession to the United States by Virginia, on March 1, 1784, of her claims north and west of the Ohio. Jefferson had already been appointed chairman of a committee to deal with the question of the future government of the western territories of the United States, and its report was brought in on the same day as the cession was completed. There was already general acceptance in Congress of the idea that the territory should be carved into new states with a view to their admittance into the Union when their population should warrant it. Jefferson's report gave a concrete form to these projects and actually provided in detail for ten new states. Typical of Jefferson were the provisions that the Governments of the new states should be republican, with no hereditary titles, and that slavery should be excluded from them after the year 1800. In the course of the debates in Congress both these points and the ten states disappeared. The ordinance of 1784 was never put into effect, but was the basis of the Northwest Ordinance of 1787. This ordinance, less democratic in its inspiration than it predecessor, not only regulated the future government of the area to which it applied, but provided a model for the political arrangements of all future territorial additions to the United States. In the ordinance of 1787, the anti-slavery proviso reappeared.

The western problem had an economic as well as a political aspect, and Jefferson was chairman of the committee which reported upon a method of surveying and disposing of the lands, and of providing for the promised grants to the soldiers of the continental army. But the solutions it proposed for the many complicated problems involved were not found acceptable, and it was another year before the first land ordinance was passed by Congress.

While post-war reconstruction and the creation of new institutions thus occupied much of Jefferson's time, he was also immersed in business arising from the foreign relations of the United States. He was chairman of a committee of three which reported, in March 1784, in favour of sending a mission to Europe to negotiate treaties of amity and commerce with those countries with which the United States still had no formal connection. The United States already had two representatives in the Old World: Benjamin Franklin, who had been minister in Paris since December 1776, and John Adams, who had been in Europe on diplomatic business since December 1779, and was now minister at The Hague. With one representative of the Middle States, and one New Englander available, it was likely that any additional member of the mission would have to come from the South, and on May 7, 1784, Jefferson was duly nominated for the vacancy.

Chapter Five
Ambassador
(1784–1789)

FOR anyone with an historical imagination, the five years which Jefferson spent in Europe must make a stronger appeal as a subject of study than any other phase of his career. Here was the philosopher of the New World confronting the Old World in the full glow of its sunset, the outspoken defender of republican simplicity accepted as a member of a highly aristocratic and sophisticated society, the representative of the newest recruit to the family of nations and one already dimly conscious of its magnificent destiny, defending its interests before the ministers of the proudest and most ancient of European monarchies. How would a political philosophy fashioned in the Capitol of colonial Williamsburg and the study at Monticello stand up to the impact of the stratified and tradition-encrusted society of the France of the Bourbons? How would Jefferson who, when he wrote so confidently of the evils of great cities, had never seen any city larger than Philadelphia—a town about the size of Bedford (in England) to-day—be struck by Paris, with its five or six hundred thousand inhabitants, or by London with its three-quarters of a million?

Unlike his successor, the able and cynical Gouverneur Morris, Jefferson kept no diary apart from his very matter-of-fact travel notes, and the complete picture of his European visit can only be constructed from his multifarious correspondence—his official and unofficial correspondence with America and his letters then, and later, to his French friends, the discovery and interpretation of which we owe largely to the researches of Professor Chinard—one of the all-too-few modern historians whose work shows an appreciation of the fact that the personal and intellectual contacts between cultures are at least as relevant to their creative activities as traffic in goods, and far more relevant than the machinations of diplomats. The eighteenth century, to which Jefferson essentially belonged, had a decent appreciation of what matters most to a society—an appreciation which the politics-crazed world of the twentieth century is rapidly losing altogether.

Jefferson's rôle in Europe was to be rather different from that which Congress had envisaged. For the triumvirate which set to work in Paris, in the summer of 1784, to prepare the framework of the new commercial relations between America and the Old World, was not of long duration. In May 1785, Adams was appointed minister to London, and in July, Franklin retired and was succeeded by Jefferson as minister to France. During his first year in Paris, Jefferson had kept very much in the background, deferring to the seniority and the greater experience of his colleagues. Now he was on his own, and with increasing responsibility came greater confidence, and a lifting of the mood of homesick depression which seems to have marred the early part of his stay.

"The succession to Dr. Franklin, at the court of France," wrote Jefferson six years later, "was an excellent school of humility. On being presented to anyone as the minister of America, the commonplace question used in such cases was, 'C'est vous, Monsieur, qui remplace le Docteur Franklin?' ('It is you, sir, who replace Doctor Franklin?') I generally answered, 'No one can replace him, sir: I am only his successor.'" Randall turned this happy conceit of Jefferson's into a brilliant impromptu by particularizing it, and making it Jefferson's reply to Vergennes, the French foreign minister and architect of the alliance which had humbled Great Britain and freed America. Subsequent biographers have of course followed Randall—although impromptus—and in French—were scarcely within Jefferson's compass. Indeed, the point of the anecdote, although rarely made, was that the remark was true. No one could have carried off for the second time the rôle of the amiable but shrewd, provincial but gallant, learned but sociable philosopher and friend which Franklin had played to such perfection on the Parisian scene. And Jefferson, even if he had been foolish enough to try, lacked some of the qualities which alone could make such a performance plausible.

"A good listener," writes Chinard, "he was much more reserved than Franklin and always remained somewhat self-conscious when he spoke or wrote French. If the Doctor spoke French as badly as he wrote it, his conversation must have been an extraordinary jargon; but Jefferson was too sensitive and had too much *amour-propre* to venture upon long discussions and conversations with people he did not know intimately. . . . We may presume that Jefferson never really felt at home in a purely French circle."

His original French friendships he owed largely to Franklin, and through them he entered into the contacts with the circle of physiocratic disciples of Turgot which were to bear fruit in his interesting later correspondence with Du Pont de Nemours and Destutt de Tracy. His other *entrée* into the intellectual and political circles opposed to the Court was provided by his acquaintance with Lafayette, whom he now met again in circumstances very different from those of beleaguered Richmond.

Throughout his mission Jefferson was at once aided and embarrassed by the wave of enthusiasm for America and the Americans which swept through the liberal and intellectual circles of France between the end of the War of Independence and the beginning of the French Revolution. It was nourished by the writings of many of the officers who had fought in America and who retained sentiments of affection for their late allies uncommon in the history of coalitions. In America, the disciples of Rousseau found, or thought they found, the exemplification of the ideal society he had portrayed, and dreamed of transferring it to their own soil. Chastellux, Crèvecœur, and others less gifted and long forgotten, contributed to building up the picture of republican simplicity, pure morals and natural piety—the amalgamated virtues of the puritan and the pioneer—which powerfully affected the French mind, and from the impression of which even the magnificent Tocqueville half a century later never completely escaped. The writings of the men of action—soldiers or pioneers—who had been to America furnished abundant inspiration to the intellectuals who had not—men like Mably and Raynal—and Jefferson was kept busy correcting the consequent flood of myth and legend, and was liable to be vexed at any moment by some Frenchman eager to advise the Americans in print how to manage their affairs on the plea that America, being mankind's hope, was therefore everybody's business.

Jefferson, in his own autobiography, made light of his diplomatic labours during these years, and it is tempting to regard them as years of observation and reflection—a second apprenticeship—rather than of active work, to linger over the records of his journeys and the technical and sociological lessons which he drew from them, as well as over his occasional lapses into æsthetic and antiquarian enthusiasm, and to ignore the tasks he was set to perform. What Jefferson considered worthy of observation we know from the rather priggishly sententious paragraphs of instruction which he penned in 1788 for the guidance of two of his compatriots. The technical achievements of each country in agriculture, architecture and such few mechanical arts as America needed were to be recorded that America might profit by it. Of "lighter mechanical arts and manufactures" he observed:

"Some of these will be worth a superficial view; but circumstances rendering it impossible that America should become a manufacturing country during the time of any man now living, it would be a waste of attention to examine them minutely."

Political and social institutions and above all
Courts which were to be seen as one "would see the
tower of London or menagerie at Versailles, with
their lions, tigers, hyenas and other beasts of prey,
standing in the same relation to their fellows," were
to be noted but only as a warning.

There were times when even the civilized and
humane Jefferson could not escape from the puri-
tanical sense of superior virtue that seems to affect
every generation that has fought a successful revolution.

His travel notes show a close approximation to
his own formula. They cover a journey to southern
France and northern Italy made between March
and June, 1787, and a tour from Paris to Amster-
dam, Strasbourg and back through Lorraine, made
in March–April 1788. Everywhere, Jefferson was
concerned with what might benefit American agriculture. Nor was he inclined to be scrupulous where
this interest was concerned. "Poggio, a muleteer,"
he noted at Vercelli on April 19, 1787," will smuggle
a sack of rough rice for me to Genoa; it being death
to export it in that form"—death for Poggio, not
for Jefferson! In writing to John Jay, the secretary
for Foreign Affairs, about his investigation into rice-
cleaning machinery and rice, Jefferson did not use
the word "smuggling," and referred diplomatically
to taking measures for obtaining a quantity of the
coveted grains. These were sent to South Carolina
and Georgia for their planters to experiment with.
"The mass of our countrymen," explained Jefferson to Jay, "being interested in agriculture, I hope

I do not err in supposing that, in a time of profound peace as the present, to enable them to adapt their productions to the market, to point out markets for them, and endeavour to obtain favorable terms of reception, is within the line of my duty."

The more conventional sides of Jefferson's line of duty can only be summarized; the problems with which he had to deal were largely those which again confronted him when he had a wider field of operations as Secretary of State after his return to America. In order to appreciate their significance, it is necessary to remember the extremely difficult position in which the new American republic found itself on the conclusion of the war.

The United States which emerged from the treaty of 1783 was by no means free of anxieties both territorial and commercial. Although the boundaries of Canada had been restored to where they had stood before 1774, and the territory between the Mississippi and Ohio rivers abandoned, the military posts which dominated this western country were still held by the British on the plea of preventing an Indian outbreak. The formal justification for ignoring this and other provisions of the Treaty was the American failure to secure the repayment of debts due to private British creditors. The efforts of Jefferson and his political associates to secure favourable action by Virginia failed in face of an opposition led by Patrick Henry. Congress was powerless to act in a matter calling for state action—an excuse which the British could not accept. But behind this controversy was the deep

American suspicion that the British had no intention of giving up their hold on the north-west, and with it the valuable fur trade upon which the commercial prosperity of Canada had been based. The old rivalry between the Hudson and the St. Lawrence, as potential outlets for the American West, revived under new political conditions. The would-be settlers and their political adherents in the United States regarded as the height of immorality a policy by which the British appeared to be maintaining the Indians as a buffer between themselves and the advancing tide of American expansion. Farther south, where the western regions of Virginia and North Carolina—the future states of Kentucky and Tennessee—were rapidly filling up, the problem was a different one. For the retention by Spain of Louisiana and New Orleans, and their acquisition of Florida (including West Florida—the coastal areas of modern Alabama and Mississippi) meant that the Mississippi outlet was more firmly than ever under Spanish control. Here Great Britain and the United States had a common interest, since they had agreed to joint navigation of the Mississippi, whose source was wrongly thought to lie in Canada. But this was not an unmixed advantage, since Great Britain might be tempted to forward her interests by the conquest of Louisiana, upon which Spain's grip was weak. Meanwhile, the life-line of the new western settlements, although open, could at any time be closed by Spanish fiat, and their future seemed mortgaged to the vicissitudes of Spanish policy. Although this fact was slow to reveal its full importance to Jefferson—like

Washington and other leaders from Virginia proper, he thought of the Potomac as the destined outlet for the West—it was to play a major part in his later thinking and diplomatic activity. What seemed of more immediate relevance was that the dispute over the northern boundary of West Florida enabled the Spaniards to play, among the Indians of the South-west, a part parallel to that of the British in the North-west; and the day in Andrew Jackson's Presidency was still far off when Tocqueville was to see the Creeks and Cherokees crossing the Mississippi on their enforced trek to their present homes in Oklahoma.

If the Americans might still regard themselves as encircled territorially, they had even more reason to fear that they would be highly vulnerable from the economic point of view. The hopes that Great Britain, their main supplier as well as their principal customer, might modify the rigours of her mercantilist doctrines in their favour proved illusory. By the Order in Council of July 2, 1783, American shipping was excluded from the British West Indies, and the staple American foodstuffs were excluded even when carried in British ships. It is true that the failure of Canada and the Maritimes to supply the deficit encouraged smuggling into the British colonies, and that trade with the colonies of other Powers became possible, so that the economic effect was less disastrous than might have been expected from a statement of the formal position. Nevertheless, the pressure to secure some more stable basis for American trade was strong, both from the growers of American exports and from the merchants who in some cases had benefitted by wartime conditions and expanded the scale of their enterprises.

In their previous dealings with foreign Powers, the Americans had always upheld, as has been seen, a very liberal view of the rights of maritime commerce, repudiating the severe position on neutral trade and contraband which Britain took up as a major sea-power. This view had been incorporated into the commercial treaty with France which had accompanied their alliance of 1778, and in the treaties with the Dutch in 1782 and with Sweden in 1783.

The task before the three commissioners in Paris in 1784 was to place on a permanent footing for the first time the relations of the United States and the majority of European Powers. The ability of the United States to bargain for commercial privileges was impaired by Congress's lack of power to make commercial regulations, and by the American adherence to the most-favoured-nation principle. But multilateral trade was essential if American commerce was to thrive, since, to take the most obvious example, the passive balance of American trade with Great Britain as re-established after the war was to some extent compensated by an active balance with France. Finally, there was the general uncertainty as to the future of the American states and of their form of government. The heavy indebtedness of the Confederation—including its big obligations to France and Holland—was a constant reminder of its lack of adequate financial resources. And although the post-war economic depression reached bottom in 1785, so that the latter years of Jefferson's stay in Europe were years of economic recovery at home, this fact was overshadowed by the political tension created by the movement towards constitutional reform, which culminated in the Philadelphia Convention of 1787.

The treaties with European states hoped for as a result of the Congressional decision of 1784 resolved themselves in the end into treaties with Prussia in 1785 and with Morocco in 1787. The acceptance by the former of the American maritime doctrines was an academic gain in view of Prussia's lack of maritime interests.

Jefferson's diplomacy as Ambassador was thus concerned with certain comparatively limited objectives. He tried and failed to get a general agreement to end the depredations of the Algerine pirates and the practice of paying them tribute by the European naval powers, nor would Congress pay the sums necessary to redeem American captives. In Jefferson's view, this was one of the occasions when resort to war would have been amply justified. He tried to break down the internal monopolies by which France and Portugal limited the value of the rights they conceded to American trade, and succeeded eventually in putting an end to the monopoly position which Robert Morris had obtained in the tobacco trade on the American side. He also eventually secured a consular convention with France. But the question to which he personally attached most importance, that of securing trading rights in the West Indian possessions of the continental Powers, proved impossible of solution. Mercantilism still dominated the policies of France, Spain and Portugal as well as of Great Britain.

In his commercial negotiations with the French court, Lafayette acted as a useful intermediary; Jefferson, who constantly took a larger view than that of particular American interests, could use with him the argument that better commercial relations would strengthen the political ties between the two countries, and that only the building up of a favourable balance of trade by the Americans would enable them to pay off their debt to France. But Lafayette came up against stiff opposition from interested parties, and as the political crisis in France became more acute, his reputation for republicanism made him a less suitable advocate.

It was this connection with Lafayette that brought Jefferson into direct contact with those who could see no way out of the difficulties with which the French monarchy was confronted, other than a radical reform of the state. Jefferson was of course in an ambiguous position as the accredited minister to Louis XVI of an allied Power, but he could not refrain from giving his advice. What is notable is that Jefferson, for all the logical rigour of his own republican and democratic creed, and in spite of the fact that all he saw in Europe convinced him of the advantages of democratic government, was not at all convinced that the French could simply take over the American institutions which they so much admired. Democracy was not merely a constitutional formula: it was a way of life—and the French might take a long time to acquire it. It was far better, he advised Lafayette in a letter written

in February 1787 at the time of the Assembly of
Notables, to take England as the model and to work
for a constitutional government, for which the
royal consent could be bought by the Assembly's
agreeing to take over the debts of the Crown. This
view, that progress for France lay along the lines
which England had travelled, was one to which
Jefferson remained constant.

After the calling of the States-General in 1789,
Jefferson again proposed a scheme by which the
French Crown should accept a constitution very
much on the British lines, but with a formal
guarantee of individual rights attached, and should
be compensated financially for the surrender of its
powers. There is evidence that even earlier than
this, Jefferson had been considering the form of a
French declaration of rights and had tried his hand
at revising a draft of Lafayette's. His comments include three points of general relevance to Jefferson's
political thought. In the first place, he emphasized
the importance of a proper adherence to the principle of the separation of powers. (One of his chief
complaints against the Constitution of Virginia had
been its failure to do this.) Secondly, he queried the
inclusion of property among the natural rights of
man: property for Jefferson was a social rather
than a natural right. Finally, he suggested a periodic
revision of the Constitution, airing for the first time
a theory to which he was later to attach much importance, that no generation has the right to bind
its successor.

Jefferson refused, as he was bound to, the invita-
tion to attend meetings of the committee set up by

the National Assembly to draft a constitution for France, but allowed his house to be used for a meeting at which the thorny question of the veto was threshed out—a breach of protocol which he hastened to avow to the French Foreign Minister Montmorin. Shortly afterwards, at the beginning of October 1789, Jefferson left France on what he hoped would be a few months' leave; he had his daughter to bring home and his 10,000 acres and 200 slaves to look after.

Jefferson was never, in fact, to revisit Europe, but the impressions he took with him were lasting ones. His affection for France was constant, and his seven weeks' visit to England in the spring of 1786 had done little to alter his preference. The French Revolution, as he had feared, brought extremists to power, and followed the classical course through complete democracy to tyranny once more. But his French friendships were unaffected by political disappointment, and Jefferson remained throughout his life the embodiment of the intellectual inter-penetration of the two great revolutions of the eighteenth century.

Chapter Six

Secretary of State
(1790–1793)

JEFFERSON'S expectations of a period of repose were not fulfilled. The new Constitution of the United States had been ratified in 1788, and on April 30, 1789, Washington was inaugurated President. Three executive departments were created by Congress—State (including home as well as foreign affairs), War and Treasury. Alexander Hamilton was suggested as Secretary of the Treasury by Robert Morris, who had until 1784 managed the Confederation's finances, but who was now increasingly absorbed in those financial speculations which were eventually to bring him to a debtor's prison. The War Department went to Henry Knox, who had been Washington's Chief of Artillery. For the Secretaryship of State, someone with experience of diplomacy was clearly needed. The aged Franklin was nearing his end; John Adams was, much to his disgust, confined to the insignificant rôle of Vice-President; John Jay, Secretary for Foreign Affairs since 1784, preferred the less onerous post of Chief Justice; the nomination of Jefferson was a foregone conclusion. His hesitations were long and genuine—his personal finances were seriously embarrassed—but in mid-February 1790, he finally accepted, and went north to join his colleagues in the new temporary capital, New York.

Jefferson was the senior of the cabinet which the fifty-eight-year-old Washington had gathered round him. He was now forty-seven; the Attorney-General, Edmund Randolph, was forty-three; Knox forty; and the brilliant and precocious Hamilton, with a considerable career of public service behind him, was thirty-three (or possibly thirty-five). Portraits and the descriptions of contemporaries enable one to picture the outward likeness of the man. Six feet two and a half inches in height, large-boned, with a reddish complexion and red hair which turned to an untidy grey, he was as rural in appearance as in tastes. His persistent shyness made him appear cold, and he had none of the glittering personal magnetism of the natural leader of men which his rival Hamilton possessed in such measure.

We have a description of him from the rather acid pen of Senator William Maclay of Pennsylvania, who wrote it after Jefferson's appearance before a Senate Committee, of which he was chairman:

"Jefferson is a slender man; has rather an air of stiffness in his manner; his clothes seem too small for him; he sits in a lounging manner, on one hip commonly, and with one of his shoulders elevated much above the other; his face has a sunny aspect; his whole figure has a loose shackling air. He had a rambling, vacant look, with nothing of that firm, collected deportment which I expected would dignify the presence of a secretary or minister. I looked for gravity, but a laxity of manner seemed shed about him. He spoke almost without ceasing; but even his discourse partook of his personal demeanour. It was loose and rambling; and yet he scattered information wherever he went, and some even brilliant sentiments sparkled from him."

Such was the man who was now entrusted with the foreign relations of the United States, and who, from within the cabinet, was to build up for himself an unequalled position as the acknowledged leader of American democracy. It is harder to draw the features of that democracy than those of Jefferson himself.

The events of the past fifteen years had altered the composition and alignment of American parties as well as the outward pattern of the United States itself. The area of settlement had grown and was continuing to grow to north and west. The population, now consisting of about four millions, including seven hundred thousand slaves, was dispersed over an area slightly larger than that of France, with its contemporary population of over twenty-six millions. As in the pre-Revolution period, the rural element in the population of the United States was still predominant, but the towns were not stationary, and New York, which almost doubled its population in the ten years after 1790, was beginning its phenomenal rise to commercial predominance.

In the distribution of wealth there had been some change. Partly this was due to causes outside the control of statesmen. The southern planters (including Jefferson himself) were being forced to abandon soil-wasting tobacco for food crops, and were in many cases (as in his own) the losers by the process. But the loss of weight in the nation with which this threatened the South as a whole was counterbalanced from 1790 onwards by the advent of the new major staple—cotton. In 1790 the cotton exports of the United States totalled 138,000 lb.; in 1800 35 million lb. The production of cotton, the purchase of new land for its cultivation and the purchase of slaves were going ahead rapidly. The application of steam to the British textile industry and the invention of the cotton-gin thus replaced Virginia by South Carolina as the leading southern state, and the change was unfortunate for Jeffersonian democracy.

But this was in the future. For the moment, the South's interests were less clearly defined, and in the recent federal convention, the South had played little part as a section except to secure the inclusion of its slaves in the formula for calculating its representation in the Federal Government. Only South Carolina and Georgia had wished to postpone the abolition of Jefferson's abomination, the African slave trade—and this was doomed to expire in 1808 in default of a major change in national sentiment.

Other changes in the internal relations of sections and classes had been effected by the war, and particularly by the massive inflation which war finance had brought about. The former wealthy class in the colonies as a whole had lost a large number of its members. Their migration to Upper Canada (Ontario) provided a new element in the complex antagonisms of the United States and Canada. But by providing the nucleus of a new agrarian economy to replace the fur trade in its domination of the St. Lawrence region, the Loyalists made possible an ultimately peaceful solution to the conflict. The whole of the colonial propertied class was not, however, destroyed by the Revolution, and it was able to absorb many new-comers, particularly those who had prospered during the hectic economic activity of the war years. Even the inflation had in some respects acted as a stimulant to economic advance, and manufacturing—the weakest link in the American economic chain—was beginning to show signs of growth. The depression which ended in 1786 had the effect of favouring the larger combinations of capital, and this tendency was accelerated by the reaching out of American commerce to more distant zones, such as the Baltic and the Far East. As a result, the process of financing through individual lending became inadequate to meet the demands of capitalist enterprise and new forms of corporate investment were evolved. The first American banks were set up in this period.

In the matter of the regulations for land-sales, other states besides Virginia passed laws which gave scope for speculative enterprise, although this did not (as Robert Morris was to find) always bring wealth to its promoters, nor did it seriously hamper the advance of pioneer settlement.

The struggle over constitution-making between conservatives and radicals in Virginia was paralleled in other states; and on the whole the conservative forces were victorious. This enabled these groups to secure commercial and fiscal legislation favourable to trade. The major struggle was over the question of the state and national debts; these had largely come into the hands of the moneyed groups, who stood out for their repayment in full in spite of the fact that they had often acquired the certificates at much below their face value. Besides this, the old colonial dispute between private debtors and creditors took on a new acerbity as prices of agricultural products fell during the deflationary period after the Peace, so that the real burden of agricultural mortgages became much more acute. The unsuccessful rising of farmer-debtors in Massachusetts in 1786, known as Shays's rebellion, arose directly from this cause, and in two states, Rhode Island and New Jersey, the radicals secured enough control of the Government to force through financial policies designed to assist debtors.

Such was the background to the problem of the federal constitution. Historians have been prone to over-simplify the issues involved. For a long time the historiography of the period was dominated by the Federalist or Hamiltonian tradition, and the period of the Confederation was depicted as one of anarchy, weakness, and economic decay, which the United States only survived thanks to its adoption of the new Constitution drawn up by the Philadelphia Convention in 1787. Since then there has been a reaction against this view. The Articles of Confederation have been regarded as on the whole successful and as reflecting, in their respect for state autonomy, the views of the radical statesmen under whom the War of Independence had been won. The movement for the adoption of the Constitution is regarded as having been something in the nature of a successful counter-revolution instigated by the moneyed groups, especially by the holders of the public debt. These are said to have hoped that a strong Federal Government would curb radical and inflationist tendencies in the states, and, by adopting a uniform commercial code, give new openings for commercial enterprise. The movement contained a strong military element—symbolized in the Society of the Cincinnati, the officers of the Revolutionary army—who anticipated new opportunities as servants of a stronger Government. The propaganda of the movement stressed the economic difficulties of the country, and the dangers of attack from abroad, and of disunion leading to the splitting up of the Confederacy at home. By painting in lurid colours the imminent triumph of extreme democratic elements and its likely consequences, these groups managed to get their way and to persuade the country to accept a new form of government under which they could prosper further. The genial propaganda of the *Federalist,* composed by Hamilton, Madison and Jay, has been accepted too freely, it is said, as a faithful picture of the times.

It is certainly true that the sentiment in favour of a modification of the Articles of Confederation was by no means unanimous. But neither the supporters nor the opponents of revision made up a single solid block. Among the former there were some certainly who despaired of the Republic; this was particularly so among army elements dissatisfied with their treatment at the hands of Congress during and after the war. But the monarchist movement was a spent force by 1789, and there seems little justification for Jefferson's long-maintained belief that his political opponents were at heart scheming to create an American Crown. On the other hand, as is shown by the project for a new Constitution which Hamilton unsuccessfully ventilated at the Convention, there was certainly a party which would have welcomed a Constitution with some nominated or hereditary element as a more permanent check to democracy. Whereas Jefferson put forward the contemporary constitution of England as a model for France to follow, Hamilton was prepared to advocate something like it for the U.S.A.

The result of the deliberations at Philadelphia, where Madison was easily the most influential single figure, was, however, much less far-reaching, and it is possible to over-emphasize the magnitude of the changes. These were mainly influenced by the views of men like Washington, who were impressed by the international weakness of the American position. The principal ones were the creation of an independent executive and the acceptance, in one House of Congress, of the principle of representation according to population, with the consequent weakening of the veto power which a small group of dissidents possessed under the old system. The granting to the central government of the sole right of regulating trade, which meant giving it at last an independent revenue, was more important for a long time to come than the limited rights of direct taxation and legislation which it also acquired.

The opposition to the ratification of the new Constitution was a heterogeneous one. To some extent the struggle followed the old lines of political cleavage, with the coastal areas favouring the Constitution, and the newer inland settlements opposed to it. But there were men who, irrespective of their economic affiliations or social interests, were disagreeably impressed by the fact that the Federal Government would come to occupy in relation to the states very much the position which the Imperial Government had held in relation to the colonies. These men were opposed to the new Constitution for the same kind of reason as had brought about the breakdown of the old system. The most prolonged debate on the Constitution was in Virginia, and it is here that the simple aristocrat-democrat, capitalist-agrarian antithesis breaks down. On one side stood Madison, John Marshall, future Secretary of State and Chief Justice, Edmund Pendleton and George Wythe; on the other, Patrick Henry, George Mason, James Monroe, one of Jefferson's closest friends and most ardent admirers, and Richard Henry Lee. The supporters of the Constitution who managed to win over Edmund Randolph, one of the delegates to Philadelphia who had refused to sign the Constitution, received their main support from the tide-water, while Henry's was still in the Piedmont. On the other hand, the Shenandoah valley frontiersmen sided with the tide-water planters and supported ratification, which would free inter-state trade and help to ensure the execution of the Treaty of Peace.

It is obvious that Jefferson's sympathies could not easily be guessed in advance. In spite of the democratic implications of his natural-rights philosophy, and of some unqualified assertions that majority rule is the basis of true republicanism, which can be culled from his writings, Jefferson never possessed the simple faith that the passing whims of majorities are always divinely inspired. His criticism of the Virginia Constitution made much of its failure properly to respect the separation of powers. He also commented unfavourably upon the fact that the two Houses of its Legislature were too homogeneous in composition:

"In some of the American States, the delegates and senators are so chosen that the first represent the persons and the second the property of the State. But with us, wealth and wisdom have an equal chance for admission into both houses. We do not therefore derive from the separation of our legislature into two houses those benefits which a proper complication of principles are capable of producing, and those which alone can compensate the evils which may be produced by their dissensions."

Such sentiments expressed in the *Notes on Virginia* might seem to foretell a ready welcome for the main principles of the new federal instrument, especially since Jefferson had ample reason to know the weaknesses of the Articles of Confederation when it came to negotiating with foreign Powers. On the other hand, he dismissed as British propaganda the assertion that the country was falling into anarchy. Shays's rebellion, which so affected the Convention, was no proof to the contrary. Its motives were "founded in ignorance not wickedness." Believing what they did, the people were right to rebel. The lethargy they would otherwise have revealed would have foreshadowed the death of liberty. . . . "What country can preserve its liberties if their rulers are not warned from time to time that their people preserve the spirit of resistance? . . . What signify a few lives lost in a century or two? The tree of liberty must be refreshed from time to time with the blood of patriots and tyrants. It is its natural manure."

Even for a private letter, this is rather strong stuff, and Jefferson's Jacobin reputation is more easily explicable if his conversation contained frequent sallies of this kind. When the text of the Constitution became available to him in France, he agreed that some of the arguments against it were not without foundation, and expected that Virginia would reject it and an improved version be proposed.

His own criticisms were revealed in letters to Madison and others. The most important, as might be expected—and one that was met in the sequel— was the omission of a formal Bill of Rights "providing clearly and without the aid of sophisms for freedom of religion, freedom of the press, protection against standing armies, restriction against monopolies, the eternal and unremitting force of the habeas corpus laws and trials by jury. . . ." The argument which James Wilson had made and which the *Federalist* was to echo—that a Government of delegated powers needs no Bill of Rights to limit its powers—did not carry weight with Jefferson. "A Bill of Rights is what the people are entitled to against every Government on earth, general or particular, and what no just Government should refuse, or rest on inferences." In the second place, he objected to the re-eligibility of the President; that, he felt, would never be denied; the post would, he felt, become one for life, with the result that foreign Powers would seek to influence the country's choice. A minor objection was that the Judiciary was not associated with the President in the exercise of his veto, nor invested with a similar and separate power. This may have been due to the conviction which he voiced in a postscript, that the Americans suffered from the instability of their laws, and that a minimum of twelve months should intervene between the introduction of a Bill and its passage into law.

In view of the fact that so much of Jefferson's later political career was taken up with his struggle with the Supreme Court, it is revealing to find that at this stage his confidence in the Judiciary had not been disturbed. "In the arguments in favor of a declaration of rights," he wrote to Madison, "you omit one which has great weight with me, the legal check which it puts into the hands of the judiciary. This is a body, which, if rendered independent and kept strictly to their own department, merits great confidence for their learning and integrity." More than a year earlier he had advocated a system of appeals from the State Courts to a Federal Court. The idea of judicial review itself was obviously familiar to Jefferson, as indeed it was to the Founding Fathers, despite the curiously common belief that it was only introduced into American constitutional practice by underhand work on the part of John Marshall. But Jefferson may not have appreciated to the full the possible extensions of judicial authority under a written constitution.

Indeed, if one takes democracy in its proper Aristotelian sense as the rule of the majority—and hence of the poor—there is little in Jefferson's criticisms of the Constitution to suggest that he was then a democrat. The title of Republican which he preferred for the party he founded was much more apt than the title of Democrat fastened on it by its opponents, and eventually, like Whig and Tory, adopted as a badge of honour by those it was meant to discredit.

For it was uncontrolled majority rule which Jefferson, like Madison, most feared. "The executive in our governments," he declared, "is not the sole, it is scarcely the principal, object of my jealousy. The tyranny of the legislatures is the most formidable dread at present, and will be for long years. That of the executive will come in its turn, but it will be at a remote period." For the true Jeffersonian, all government was suspect: "I own I am not a friend to a very energetic government. It is always oppressive."

The eventual adoption of a Bill of Rights removed Jefferson's principal misgivings about the Constitution, and when he returned to the United States, it was in a mood of confidence about his country's political future. It would thus be a mistake to think that Washington included Jefferson in his cabinet in order to create within it a definite party balance. The party division in 1790 was between the supporters and the opponents of the new Constitution, between Federalists and anti-

Federalists. Jefferson's position in this was quite clear: writing from Paris as early as March 13, 1789, he said:

"I am not a Federalist, because I never submitted the whole system of my opinions to the creed of any party of men whatever, in religion, in philosophy, in politics, or in anything else where I was capable of thinking for myself. Such an addiction is the last degradation of a free and moral agent. If I could not go to heaven but with a party, I would not go there at all. Therefore I protest to you I am not of the party of federalists. But I am much farther from that of the anti-federalists. . . . I am of neither party, nor yet a trimmer between parties."

There was, then, nothing in recent events to make it impossible for Jefferson to work in harmony with Hamilton as the guiding spirits of the new administration. Their estrangement and conflict which formed the essence of the political history of the years 1790–93 were the result of happenings subsequent to Jefferson's taking up office. In the autobiographical fragments known as the *Anas*, Jefferson ascribes his opposition to Hamilton as dating from his discovery, on his arrival at New York, of the strongly anti-Republican tone which permeated administration circles; but it seems probable that the parting of the ways was a more gradual one than this account suggests.

The divergences between Jefferson's political creed and Hamilton's showed themselves in relation to the practical problems which confronted Washington's cabinet during his first administration. These had both an internal and an external aspect.

But the two were closely connected. Hamilton's aim was to strengthen the newly formed Government and to link its fortunes to those of the commercial classes. The basis of this was to be the creation of a sufficient revenue. This in turn could only be done by securing a large sum from the Customs, which presupposed a big volume of foreign trade. Under the existing circumstances, the only quick way towards this was to rebuild, as rapidly as possible, American trade with Great Britain. This meant good political relations with Great Britain even at the expense of legitimate American claims. Thus Hamilton's policy, as Secretary of the Treasury, inevitably led him to try to influence—and even, by clandestine dealings with British representatives, actively to interfere with—the work of his colleague's department. The French Revolution introduced a new ideological complication, since Hamilton's pro-British policy was ascribed by Jefferson to his fondness for the British form of government, while Jefferson's wish to maintain the French alliance was ascribed to a latent sympathy with revolutionary doctrines.

The ideological issue also separated Jefferson for the first time from his old collaborator John Adams. The latter had regarded the new Constitution as subject to criticism from the point of view of the weakness under it of the Executive; and by his publication when already Vice-President of a highly academic political treatise, the *Discourses on Davila,* he laid himself open to the familiar charge of covert monarchism. The publication in 1791 of Paine's *Rights of Man* and a further outburst of ideological polemics served to widen the breach between those who welcomed and those who feared events in France. By this time, Jefferson—who, like Hamilton, was dabbling in the dangerous game of influencing the press—had clumsily laid himself open to the charge of being foremost among Adams's detractors. On the other hand, Hamilton, whatever his private views, was not thankful to Adams for giving the opposition a ground on which to attack the tendencies within the administration which he represented, and the Federalist party was soon split by their personal rivalry. Jefferson, on the other hand, rapidly secured as an ally James Madison, the real progenitor of the Constitution, and Hamilton's collaborator in the *Federalist*. He was the leading member in the House of Representatives, a body not yet overshadowed by the Senate as in later times. Thus, within a few years, the Federalist party had shed one wing—the Virginian—and the national coalition of the American Revolution was at an end. On the other hand, Jefferson and Madison now received support from the old anti-Federalists, from those who had opposed the new Constitution, but now opposed Hamiltonian innovations in its name. These were partly Southern agrarians, opposing Hamilton's favours for the moneyed classes in the name of States Rights, partly frontiersmen objecting to the neglect of the West and its problems in the search for commercial privilege, and partly the popular party in the Middle States, such as the followers of Hamilton's New York rival, George Clinton.

From this point of view the last ten years of the eighteenth century in the United States stand out as those of the creation of a two-party system as the motive power in a constitutional system which itself knew nothing of parties, and which was to some extent designed to discourage them. But it was also a period of national emancipation after the perils of the Confederate period, and the work of the Government, both internally and externally, commands attention.

The internal policies of the Washington administration were the policies of Hamilton; and Jefferson's rôle was primarily that of a critic and objector. By the time Jefferson took up office, Hamilton had already made some progress in the task of re-establishing the nation's finances and funding its external and internal debt. The main question still in debate was that of the state debts which Hamilton wished to see taken over by the Federal Government, largely for the political reason that the prosperity of the investing classes would thereby be more closely bound up with the stability of the régime. This proposal met considerable opposition from those who argued that, to fund these debts at par would be to put large profits into the hands of those who had bought them up at low prices from the original creditors. It was also a fact that some states, particularly Virginia, which had paid off the bulk of their debts would be taxed by this measure for the benefit of the less punctilious.

The matter was finally settled by a bargain between the two Secretaries. Jefferson and his supporters in Congress agreed to accept the Assumption Bill, provided that the capital of the Union (after an interval of ten years during which it should be at Philadelphia) was finally located in southern territory on the shore of the Potomac. Jefferson later regretted this concession, which had thrown twenty millions of stock "as a pabulum to the stock-jobbing herd" and "added to the number of votaries to the Treasury," and in the *Anas* he did his best to minimize his share in the transaction.

Even more contrary to Jefferson's fundamental position was Hamilton's proposal that Congress should charter a National Bank with powers to issue notes and to lend to the Federal Government. Jefferson described himself as "unversed in financial projects and calculations and budgets." But if he had few theoretical opinions on strictly economic matters, he had, like many other people similarly circumstanced, very strong prejudices; and among these was one against paper money in any form. "Paper," he had remarked in connection with British finance, "is poverty . . . it is only the ghost of money and not money itself." This "hard money" view was consistently maintained by Jefferson, and appears again in his comments in 1816 on the proposed Second Bank of the United States. Like Andrew Jackson after him, Jefferson had to cope with a wing in his party whose predominantly debtor position led them to favour paper money and a progressive inflation, but like Jackson's his own instincts were strongly on the other side.

Furthermore, the proposed Bank would again strengthen the Hamiltonian party, adding to its following a "mercenary phalanx" in Congress bound by ties of interest to the Treasury and its system. Like another of Hamilton's proposed measures, the Excise Bill which passed into law in 1791, the establishment of the Bank would provide new opportunities for Treasury patronage. The existence of a large class of people wholly or partially dependent for their livelihood upon the Federal Government, or upon an institution so closely connected with it as a National Bank, was the very antithesis of republican government as Jefferson conceived it.

For the root of Jefferson's opposition to the Hamiltonian programme was political rather than economic. Hamilton's "system," wrote Jefferson to Washington in a letter expounding his position in September, 1792, "flowed from principles adverse to liberty, and was calculated to undermine and demolish the republic by creating an influence of his department over the members of the legislature." Furthermore, two at least of Hamilton's measures, the Bank Bill and the unsuccessful proposal for a protective tariff, seemed to Jefferson to violate the principles of the new Constitution as he understood them.

Washington himself had had constitutional scruples about signing the Bank Bill, and before finally overcoming them he had asked both Hamilton and Jefferson to give him their opinions in writing on the question of the constitutionality of the measure. From Hamilton's opinion, it is clear that he regarded the Federal Government as one possessing only certain powers, it is true, but within those powers supreme. For, he said, "this *general principle* is *inherent* in the very definition of government, and *essential* to every step of the progress to be made by that of the United States, namely: That every power vested in a government is in its nature *sovereign,* and includes by *force* of the *term,* a right to employ all the *means* requisite and fairly applicable to the attainment of the *ends* of such power, and which are not precluded by restrictions and exceptions specified in the constitution, or not immoral, or not contrary to the *essential ends* of political society."

By reasoning of this kind, and with the aid of the "general welfare" clause of the Constitution, the right to charter a bank could be deduced from the power to tax.

For Jefferson, however, the "general welfare" clause conveyed no such far-reaching powers. Congress could not do *"anything they please* to provide for the general welfare," but only lay taxes for the purpose, and to charter a bank was not to lay a tax. Otherwise, he observed, the whole point of enumerating the powers of the Federal Government would be lost. The Constitution would be reduced to "a single phrase, that of instituting a Congress with power to do whatever would be for the good of the United States, and as they would be the sole judge of the good or the evil, it would also be a power to do whatever evil they please."

Another method by which the Constitution could be manipulated to convey to Congress more than the powers specifically enumerated was by a broad interpretation of its power "to make all laws which shall be necessary and proper for carrying into execution" the specific powers vested in the Federal authority. Jefferson argued that "necessary" in this context meant essential and not simply convenient. Unless a specified power could not be exercised without the extra power demanded, there was no constitutional authority for it; and clearly a National Bank was not an essential prerequisite for exercising the power to tax. In Jefferson's view, the Bank Bill was further assailable, in that its powers involved overriding certain of "the most ancient and fundamental laws of the several states."

The issues raised in the controversy transcended the immediate question of the bank, and continued to be agitated after the Bill was signed by Washington. For they revealed that the new Constitution was capable of presenting very different aspects according to how it was interpreted. Over this, the authors of the *Federalist* were themselves split. Hamilton and Jay were among those who held that what had been created at Philadelphia was a truly national government, possessing the inherent rights of a sovereign power and responsible for using them to the full for the public benefit, subject only to the specific limitations imposed by its federal form. Madison interpreted the new Constitution, like the old Articles of Confederation, as a bargain between sovereign states who had delegated to a central authority such powers of government as could best be exercised collectively, but who had no intention of thereby surrendering their individuality or their primary responsibility to their own citizens. Such was also the view of Jefferson. The notions of rights and of contract which were the basis of his theory of political obligation were transferred from the individual to the corporate sphere. Instead of a social contract between individuals, there was a contract between societies, and the societies in question—the States—had no more surrendered their rights to the Union than men had surrendered their natural rights when they entered into society. The concept of divided sovereignty had enabled this fundamental divergence to be overcome at the time of the Convention, but as soon as different interests began to form into parties, the dilemma reappeared. It was not to disappear again during Jefferson's lifetime, nor for many decades to come.

It is against this background of growing friction within the cabinet that Jefferson's own work at the Department of State falls to be considered. As has been seen, the new Government inherited from the old Congress a series of unresolved problems primarily affecting relations with Great Britain and Spain. Jefferson's own views before taking office were on the whole in favour of doing nothing to precipitate matters. The Europe in which he had been living had seemed to him one vast powder-keg. At any moment an explosion might be precipitated and the Great Powers once more come to grips. In such circumstances the United States might bargain between Great Britain and Spain and throw the weight of its favourable neutrality (talk of war was bluff) into the balance in return for the granting of its claims.

In 1790, the lines of British and Spanish expansion converged at Nootka Sound, on the Pacific Coast of North America. At one moment this seemed almost certain to precipitate war. Jefferson was of the opinion that the occasion could be used by the Americans to extract from Spain the grant of the freedom of navigation on the Mississippi which she had denied, and with it, a port for the transhipment of goods, without which the right of navigation would be valueless. But Jefferson was unwilling at this period to endanger Spain's feeble hold over the bulk of her nominal territories in the Americas. As early as 1786 he had written home:

"We should take care not to think it for the interest of that great continent to press too soon on the Spaniards. Those countries cannot be in better hands. My fear is that they are too feeble to hold them till our population can be sufficiently advanced to gain it from them piece by piece. The navigation of the Mississippi we must have. This is all we are yet ready to receive."

These fears became actual when it was thought probable that, in the event of war, Britain might attempt the conquest of Louisiana and Florida, and request passage for British troops through American territory. Washington put the hypothetical question to his cabinet, and received very uncertain counsel, although Hamilton advocated an American expedition against New Orleans and a British alliance at the expense of American claims against Britain in the matter of the northern forts. Jefferson's own voice was raised in favour of temporizing and of acquiescing if necessary in the *fait accompli*. He advised, however, that the United States should let it be known that it would view "with extreme uneasiness any attempt of either power to seize the possessions of the other" upon the United States borders, since the United States' own safety was "interested in a due balance between our neighbours." Thus Jefferson voiced, perhaps for the first time, the view that all changes in the location of power on the American continent were a proper matter of concern to the United States—a view which may be regarded as the original germ of the Monroe Doctrine.

The Anglo-Spanish crisis passed without war, and the Americans were driven back upon the ordinary course of diplomacy. Jefferson had by now become one of the warmest advocates of settling the question of the Mississippi navigation. From the national point of view, it was indeed increasingly clear that only some solution of this kind could keep the trans-Alleghanian settlements—the new states of Kentucky (1792) and Tennessee (1796)— permanently within the Union. Furthermore, if one accepts the view that Jefferson had by now definitely embarked upon building up a rival party to the dominant Hamiltonian Federalists, the issue was one which he could not neglect. The northern states had been won over for Hamilton's financial and commercial policy; it was necessary to outbid Patrick Henry for the allegiance of the South and West.

The arguments with which Jefferson pressed the American case—to deaf ears as it proved—are an interesting illustration of the way in which his thinking on international questions was blended of the conventional historical and legal arguments propounded with much casuistry, and of theories of natural rights which were in fact peculiar to Jefferson himself.

They are best studied in his instructions to William Short, one of his envoys to Spain, which were drawn up on March 18, 1792. In these he argued with complete assurance that the inhabitants of riparian states have a universal right to the navigation of rivers beyond their own borders. If one appeals to the law of Nature and Nations—the two notions were never very clearly differentiated in Jefferson's thinking—as one finds it "written in the heart of man, what sentiment is written in deeper characters than that the Ocean is free to all men, and the Rivers to all their inhabitants?" The rhetorical question happily ignored current practice. Nor was there much greater force in the argument that the right of navigation gives the right to facilities on the shore on the principle that "the means follow their end."

Natural rights also furnished a ground for Jefferson's equally unsuccessful attempts to secure modifications in foreign commercial codes. Who can avoid, he had asked Washington in 1788, seeing the cause of a possible future war "in the tyranny of those nations who deprive us of the natural right of trading with our neighbours?" And in a letter in 1791, dealing with French restrictions on the imports of American tobacco, he declared that "an exchange of surpluses and wants between neighbouring nations is both a right and a duty under the moral law, and measures against right should be mollified in their exercise." Neither Great Britain nor France was prepared to accept Jefferson's

interpretation of the moral law, but Jefferson had
come into office with the firm conviction that
France had earned particular favours from the
United States. Britain, on the other hand, was the
country which had "moved heaven, earth and hell
to exterminate" the Americans in war, insulted
them "in all her councils in peace," shut her doors
to them "in every part where her interest would
admit it," libelled them in foreign nations, and endeavoured to poison them against receiving the
Americans' "most precious commodities." The idea
that gratitude was not a proper foundation for national policy was one which had been "buried for
centuries with its kindred principles of the lawful-
ness of assassination, poison, perjury, etc."

The arguments in favour of better relations with
Great Britain were in fact too strong to be ignored.
But the possibility of securing British friendship on
America's terms was not great. During the Nootka
Sound crisis, the British were rather more careful of
American susceptibilities; but this did not prevent
them from considering Levi Allen's overtures for
the recognition of the independence of Vermont.
Congress soon exercised its powers under the new
Constitution to pass tariff and navigation Acts; but
Madison's attempt to use the opportunity to dis-
criminate against British goods was defeated by
Hamilton's influence in Congress. On the other
hand, the moderate preferences incorporated in the
Acts of 1789 and 1790 did something to help American shipping and make up for the fact that Ameri-
can-built ships which had previously formed a large
proportion of the British mercantile marine were

now reckoned as foreign even if in British ownership. The existence of these laws also made it necessary for Great Britain to reverse her previous policy
of being unrepresented at Philadelphia. Both her
first (unofficial) envoy, Beckwith, and his successor
George Hammond, who arrived in November 1791
as the first British minister to the United States,
established close contacts with Hamilton, and
worked with him to try to get over the obstacles to
Anglo-American trade.

Hammond put forward, in his negotiations with
Jefferson, the standard British view that the retention of the northern forts and other matters complained of was due to American violations of the
peace treaty. Jefferson's reply, dated May 29, 1792,
a document of about 17,000 words, has been described by an American student of his diplomacy,
Professor S. F. Bemis, "as his greatest diplomatic
note, and indeed one of the cleverest arguments in
the history of American diplomacy . . . a monument to the man's capacity for work, to his infinite
pains and to his legal acumen," and he blames
Hamilton's intervention for its practical ineffectiveness and for Jefferson's failure to advance the
British negotiations by a single step during his
tenure of the Secretaryship of State. In the north-
west, the British held to their positions, and the
spectre of a Red Indian barrier state receiving back-
ing from Canada continued to haunt the American
mind, in spite of its abandonment by the British
Government as early as August 1792. The complex
question of the Indians, their opposition to further
settlement and consequent suspicion of the Ameri-

cans were indeed major preoccupations of Jefferson's. Even apart from possible British assistance to the Indians, military measures against them were difficult and costly. Writing to Monroe in April 1791, he said:

"I hope we shall drub the Indians well this summer and then change our plan from war to bribery. We must do as the Spaniards and English do, keep them in peace by liberal and constant presents. They find it the cheapest plan and so shall we. . . . In this way hostilities being suspended for some length of time, a real affection may succeed on our frontiers to that hatred now existing there. Another powerful motive is that in this way we may leave no pretext for raising or continuing an army. Every rag of an Indian depredation will otherwise serve as a ground to raise troops with those who think a standing army and a public debt necessary for the happiness of the U.S. and we shall never be permitted to get rid of either."

Arguments around the question of who first violated the treaty of 1783 and the other familiar items in the list of Anglo-American differences became of secondary concern as the French Revolution began to exercise its powerful influence, not only on internal American politics, but on international alignments as well. So long as the war waged by revolutionary France concerned only the land Powers—the Empire and Prussia—American interests were unaffected. But after the execution of Louis XVI, the new Republic declared war on the maritime Powers, Great Britain, Holland and Spain. When early in April 1793 this news reached the American

Government, it was, although not unexpected, bound to cause concern. The whole basis of Jefferson's previous policy was undermined. Instead of a war between Great Britain and Spain allowing the Americans freedom of manœuvre, Great Britain and Spain were now fighting in a common cause, and were soon formally allied in the First Coalition. In the second place, there was the question as to how far the United States was itself committed by its old treaty of alliance with France.

Washington was strongly in favour of complete neutrality, but once again consulted his cabinet on the line to be pursued, and particularly, on whether a proclamation of neutrality should be issued, and whether a minister from the French Republic should be received and full recognition thus granted to the new régime. Hamilton argued that the operation of the treaty had been modified by the change of régime, since it had been made with the French monarchy. Otherwise it might oblige the United States to help prevent a Restoration. Furthermore, the treaty had been concluded as a defensive alliance, and since it was France which had declared war against Great Britain and Spain, she was not entitled to claim its benefits. On the other hand, he accepted the Republic's claim to the debt still owed by the United States to France. What he advocated was that the reception of the new French minister should be accompanied by some declaration to the effect that the United States held the operation of the treaties of 1778 to be in suspense. If not, Great Britain would be justified in treating the United States as an enemy.

Jefferson's views were of course very different, although he did not recommend more than a favourable neutrality towards France. He had previously made it clear that for him there could be no question of the French Republic's right to recognition. The right of every people to change its form of government as often as it desired was a fundamental. Indeed, he had on at least one occasion voiced his doubts as to whether any generation has the right to bind its successors—a doubt which it is difficult to reconcile with his favouring of written Constitutions and Bills of Rights.

In December 1792, he wrote to Gouverneur Morris, American minister to France:

"We surely cannot deny to any nation that right whereon our own government is founded, that every one may govern itself under whatever form it pleases, and change these forms at its own will; and that it may transact its business with foreign nations through whatever organ it thinks proper, whether King, convention, assembly, committee, President, or whatever else it may choose. The will of the nation is the only thing essential to be regarded."

Jefferson held that there was no present need to renounce the treaties. The clause permitting French ships and privateers to use American ports was unlikely to cause trouble; the United States were not bound to grant France the right to fit out privateers in American ports, although they had explicitly promised to withhold such permission from France's enemies. There was no certainty that France, which the Americans had not asked to intervene over the

British retention of their posts in the north-west, would insist on their intervening in the West Indies. In the last of his suppositions he was correct. What France wanted was a benevolent neutrality; American supplies, both in the West Indies and at home, would be more useful than such active help as the United States' limited resources might allow it to give. Jefferson's argument that the United States need not at once denounce the treaty was sound enough; on the other hand, if it came to a showdown, Jefferson, like Hamilton, would risk war with France rather than with Great Britain.

Washington's so-called neutrality proclamation of April 22, 1793—one of the cardinal documents of American foreign policy—bore marks of Jefferson's influence in two important particulars. In the first place, the word "neutrality" was studiously omitted from the text, which referred only to "friendly and impartial" conduct towards the belligerents. In the second place, the United States' withdrawal of protection from those of its citizens engaged in trading with the belligerents was confined to those carrying articles "deemed contraband by the *modern usage* of nations." This indicated that the Americans would insist on upholding the view, which Great Britain consistently denied, that foodstuffs were not contraband. Their position received added importance from France's opening, in February 1793, of her ports, both at home and in the colonies, to United States shipping and the exemption, in May, of the United States from French measures against neutral trade with Great Britain. In June 1793, on the other hand, a British Order-in-Council authorized the detention of all neutral vessels laden with provisions and the compulsory sale of their cargoes in British ports, and further severe measures were taken in the following November. These were modified in January 1794 so as to allow the United States to continue in those trades which it had been permitted to carry on in peace-time—an application of the so-called rule of 1756.

The British Order-in-Council of 1793 marked the beginning of the active phase of the long struggle by the United States to get its broad views on the rights of neutral shipping accepted in time of war by foreign belligerents. This issue—undecided when the cycle of Anglo-French wars drew to an end in 1815—was strikingly renewed when the Anglo-German conflict began in 1914.

The question was also influenced by the prodigious growth of American shipping in the period immediately after 1789—a growth which profoundly affected the economic and political outlook of New England. In 1790 American ships carried under half of the trade between the United States and Great Britain; in 1800 nearly 95 per cent. The registered tonnage of the American mercantile marine was 124,000 tons in 1789, 365,000 tons in 1793 and over half a million tons in 1800—over three-quarters of a million if the rapidly increasing coastal, whaling and fishing fleets are taken into account.

One other important point in the President's proclamation is of interest from the point of view of Jefferson's position. This is the omission of Spain from the list of the belligerents to which it was to apply. It appears that Jefferson's scruples about the possible results of the break-up of Spain's empire had been overcome, and that he was now prepared to countenance a French-backed revolt, provided that the Floridas could be acquired for the United States. But further involvement in these projects was prevented by Washington's fears that Great Britain would come to Spain's aid, and that the French designs would involve the United States in the war with Great Britain which it was the whole purpose of his policy to avoid.

Jefferson himself wrote of the pusillanimity of the proclamation, but his difficulties in working the policy and the conduct of the new French minister, Citizen Edmond Genêt, were to prove important arguments in favour of caution. For Genêt's instructions, while they looked ultimately to the negotiation of a new treaty linking more closely the fortunes of the French and American Republics, also authorized him to take measures in anticipation of it. He intrigued with restless elements in Kentucky to raise revolt in Spanish Louisiana, and made plans for George Rogers Clark to lead an expedition against New Orleans by land, to coincide with a naval attack. He issued proclamations to the inhabitants of Louisiana and of Canada and Nova Scotia, commissioned privateers and set up a French prize court. The enthusiastic reception which he received from some pro-French elements, on his arrival in the United States in May 1793, was not matched in government circles. British protests against his activities warned the administration of the dangers into which it was running, and Jefferson sharply reminded Genêt of the United States' neutral position. Jefferson's early cordiality towards the Frenchman gave way to keen dislike, when the envoy took it upon himself to lecture him on his duties and to treat Washington himself in similar arrogant fashion. In August, Jefferson formally requested the French Government to recall Genêt. By this time, however, the Girondins, Genêt's party, had been swept out of power in France, and their leaders guillotined. Their Jacobin successors saw no objection to recalling Genêt, and sent with the new minister an order for his arrest. To return to France would mean the guillotine, and now that Genêt was harmless, there was no reason to gratify the blood-lust of France's rulers. Genêt, who had meanwhile married a daughter of the powerful New York politician George Clinton, was allowed to forget his revolutionary past as a respectable citizen of the United States with strong interests in agriculture and science.

The attention of Jefferson was divided in 1793 between preventing Genêt from providing Great Britain with strong reasons for complaint of American conduct, and protesting to Great Britain against the ignoring of American interests and views in her policy at sea. In the latter task he was handicapped, partly by Hamilton's continued contacts with Hammond, which led Great Britain to believe that Jefferson's formal objections need not be taken too seriously, but still more by the fact that a power as weak as the United States from the naval point of view was in no position to make the British moderate the use of their main weapon. For nearly a quarter of a century British sea-power was the major obstacle to the ambitions, first of revolutionary and then of Napoleonic France. It was an obstacle which third-party appeals to the law of nations and of nature could not be expected to affect.

Although Jefferson had played a leading part in urging Washington to allow himself to be re-elected in 1792, he came increasingly to dislike the minority position which he occupied in the cabinet, and to resent the interference of Hamilton in matters outside the province of his department. The open warfare carried out on behalf of Hamilton and Jefferson by the two newspaper editors whom they respectively subsidized, Fenno of the *Gazette of the United States* and Freneau of the *National Gazette,* did little credit to either. Jefferson was too sensitive to criticism to enjoy the contest. In a letter while still in Paris, he had numbered among the advantages of the post he then held the lack of publicity with which it was attended. "My great wish," he wrote, "is to go on in a strict but silent performance of my duty; to avoid attracting notice and to keep my name out of the newspapers, because I find the pain of a little censure, even when it is unfounded, is more acute than the pleasure of much praise." When Washington attempted to moderate the polemics of his two Secretaries, Jefferson replied (in September 1792) in a long and bitter letter which concluded with an announcement of his intention to retire at the end of Washington's first term in the following March. Washington and Madison managed to persuade him to change his mind. Further requests to be allowed to resign were overruled by

the President during 1793, but on the last day of
the year Jefferson had his wish and left office, being
succeeded by his fellow-Virginian, the Attorney-
General, Edmund Randolph. On January 16, 1794,
Jefferson, once more a private citizen, arrived back
at Monticello. Although only fifty years old, he felt
himself exhausted by his long years of public service, and regarded himself as destined to pass his
remaining years in retirement, occupying himself
with the care of his estates, his library and his
family. Of his two daughters, of whom he had seen
little since he had come back with them from Paris,
the elder, Martha, was married to Thomas Mann
Randolph, who had been managing Jefferson's
estates, and was the mother of a son, Thomas Jefferson Randolph—the favourite grandchild of Jefferson's old age. The younger daughter, Maria, now
aged sixteen, stayed at home until her marriage in
1797 to her cousin John Wayles Eppes. Jefferson's
correspondence for 1794 and 1795 is so scanty as to
suggest that his family and his Virginia friends were
company enough. Even his subscriptions to the
Philadelphia newspapers were discontinued, although his knowledge of the course of public affairs
was kept up to date by letters from the two Virginian leaders of the anti-Hamiltonian party in
Congress, James Madison and W. B. Giles.

Chapter Seven

In Opposition
(1794–1800)

THE years 1794–6, which Jefferson spent without
moving above seven miles from Monticello,
living, as he described himself, like "an Antedi-
luvian patriarch" among his children and grandchildren, and tilling his soil, were years of great
importance in the history of his country and of the
western world. While Jefferson strove to restore his
fortunes by starting a nail-factory which employed
a "dozen little boys from 10 to 16 years of age," and
experimented with a new plough of his own design,
the French Revolution reached and passed its
climax. The year 1793 had seen the ascent of Robespierre. It was he who, in November of that year,
finally committed revolutionary France to an all-
out struggle with England, based on the hope that
the Revolution would engulf that country likewise,
but relying meanwhile upon the argument of force
—all-out warfare on the Continent and a strongly
protectionist economic policy, the forerunner of the
Napoleonic "continental system." In July 1794,
Robespierre fell. The counter-revolution began and
gathered speed. In the spring and summer of 1795,
Prussia, Spain and some of the minor allies were
detached from the Coalition, which now consisted
substantially of England and Austria alone. The
Convention was allowed to bring into being a Con-

stitution under which France for four years enjoyed a foretaste of nineteenth-century middle-class constitutionalism. But the "normalcy," which was what the Directory implied for many Frenchmen, did not return to Europe. The attempts of the Directory to bring about a general pacification were unsuccessful. It was Bonaparte's Italian campaign of 1796–7 that brought Austria to admit defeat. By the time that Bonaparte signed the preliminary peace of Loeben in April 1797 leaving only England (and Portugal) to maintain the struggle, Jefferson was back in Philadelphia as Vice-President of the United States.

The reactions of Jefferson to the transformation of the French Revolution from a liberating force to one which itself threatened the liberties of nations deserve study. The comments on European events which appear in his letters show that it was ultimately their repercussions in his own country which concerned him. He was the less likely to condemn what he disapproved, because any fall in French popularity was bound to enhance the reputation of Hamilton and other "Anglomen."

It must be admitted, that despite the caution which he had shown when in France, and the warnings which he had uttered against a too-ready assumption that France was ready for democracy, the Revolution acquired a more pronounced element of glamour once he was back on the other side of the Atlantic. Burke's *Reflections on the French Revolution* merely led him to exclaim that it was "mortifying that this evidence of the rottenness of his mind" obliged one now "to ascribe to

151

wicked motives those actions of his life which bore the mark of virtue and patriotism." In January 1793, he protested in a letter to William Short against the latter's censure of the Jacobins in his despatches from Holland. In the struggle which was necessary, for their victory, he wrote:

"Many guilty persons fell without the forms of trial, and with them some innocent. These I deplore as much as anybody and shall deplore some of them to the day of my death. But I deplore them as I should have done had they fallen in battle. It was necessary to use the arm of the people, a machine not quite so blind as balls and bombs, but blind to a certain degree. . . . My own affections have been deeply wounded by some of the martyrs to this cause, but rather than it should have failed, I would have seen half the earth desolated. Were there but an Adam and Eve left in every country and left free, it would be better than as it now is."

The reason for this unusually bloodthirsty reflection is clearly to be found in party sentiment. What Jefferson was concerned with was the defeat of the American party, which he persisted in regarding as monarchist: "The successes of republicanism in France have given a *coup de grâce* to their prospects and I hope to their projects."

In a letter to his son-in-law a few days later, he developed the same theme:

"Our news from France continues to be good and to promise a continuance. The event of the revolution there is now little doubted of, even by its enemies (i.e. the abolition of the monarchy in September 1792). The sensation it has produced here, and the indications of them in the public papers, have shown that the form our own government was to take depended much more on the events of France than anybody had before imagined. The tide, which after our former relaxed government took a violent course toward the opposite extreme, and seemed ready to hang everything round with the tassels and baubles of monarchy, is now getting back as we hope to a just mean, a government of laws addressed to the reason of the people, and not to their weaknesses."

In a letter in May 1793, Jefferson emphasized the importance of the United States keeping clear of "the European combustion," particularly in view of the critical situation with regard to the Indians, in both the North-west and the South. The question was—would the warring powers permit the United States to stand aloof?

"This they will do probably if France is successful; but if great successes were to attend the arms of the kings, it is far from certain they might not chuse to finish their job completely, by obliging us to change in the form of our government at least, a change which would be grateful to a party here not numerous but influential. . . . This summer is of immense importance to the future condition of mankind all over the earth, and not a little to ours. For though its issue should not be marked by any direct change in our constitution, it will influence the tone and principles of its administration, so as to lead it to something very different in the one event from what it would be in the other."

By June, the conduct of the French was beginning

to alarm Jefferson, who wrote (again to Randolph): "The French have been guilty of great errors in their conduct towards other nations, not only in insulting uselessly all crowned heads, but endeavouring to force liberty on their neighbours in their own form." But Jefferson consoled himself with the reflection that on the latter point they were correcting themselves; and even Genêt's disastrous course did not fundamentally alter his pro-French attitude.

The fortunes of the French continued to occupy Jefferson's mind during his retirement, and once again his enthusiasm outweighed his caution.

"Over the foreign powers," he wrote, "I am convinced they will triumph completely, and I cannot but hope that that triumph, and the consequent disgrace of the invading tyrants, is destined, in the order of events, to kindle the wrath of the people of Europe against those who have dared to embroil them in such wickedness, and to bring at length kings, nobles and priests to the scaffolds which they have been so long deluging with human blood."

In April 1795, when there appeared the possibility of a general peace between France and her enemies on the Continent, Jefferson wrote that if this could be achieved, he would have "little doubt of dining with Pichegru in London next autumn." For, he continued, "I believe I should be tempted to leave my clover for awhile to go and hail the dawn of liberty and republicanism in that island." The revolution in Holland and the close association between that country and France aroused Jefferson to new transports of joy. In a letter on June 1, 1795, he wrote: "This ball of liberty, I believe most piously, is now so well in motion that it will roll round the globe. At least the enlightened part of it, for light and liberty go together. It is our glory that we first put it into motion, and our happiness that, being foremost, we had no bad example to follow. What a tremendous obstacle to future attempts at liberty will be the atrocities of Robespierre." That the cause of France was still the cause of Liberty, Jefferson saw no reason to doubt.

In his views on France, Jefferson no doubt represented the majority of the Republican party which had made considerable headway in Congress in the elections of 1792 and 1794. Indeed, Jefferson considered the anti-Republicans in the house to be now only a weak minority, although admitting that the slower rate of change in the composition of the Senate had prevented it following so closely the course of popular opinion. By now, Jefferson's earlier expressed aversion from party had disappeared:

"Were parties here divided merely by a greediness for office, as in England, to take part with either would be unworthy of a reasonable or moral man, but where the principle of difference is as substantial and as strongly pronounced as between the Republicans and the Monocrats of our country, I hold it as honorable to take a firm and decided part, and as immoral to pursue a middle line, as between the parties of Honest Men and Rogues into which every country is divided."

The employment of military force to deal with the Pennsylvania riots against the excise, the so-called "Whisky rebellion," had seemed to Jefferson a further proof of Hamilton's dark designs of "strengthening government and increasing the public debt." Suggestions of legislative action against the pro-French "democratic societies" caused a further denunciation of "the servile copyist of Mr. Pitt," whose resignation, on January 31, 1795, did not diminish his influence with the President and with his party.

But with so little scope for controversy over internal politics, it was foreign affairs that provided the main fuel for the flames of party, and it was the Republicans' misfortune that the Directory, inheriting Robespierre's legacy of commercial warfare, were not willing to play their game to the hoped-for extent. The truth was that both sides in the war at sea were equally indifferent to anything but their own advantage, and as Professor Bemis has pointed out: "Really the United States Government did treat the French spoliations, which were in violation of a treaty, more indulgently than the British, which were not."

From the point of view of American public opinion, the French gained from the fact that they could not for obvious reasons adopt the British practice of searching American ships for real or alleged deserters from the British Navy. The British naval mutinies of 1797 focused attention on the conditions under which the imperilled men would be serving. Successive Secretaries of State from Jefferson onwards sought unsuccessfully to find a solution to the problem which conflicting concepts of citizenship and conflicting views on the right of expatriation made doubly difficult.

In December 1793, Madison reintroduced into Congress the proposed regulations of 1791 discriminating against British trade. The Federalists opposed this, pointing out that United States trade with Great Britain was now four-fifths of the total, while for Great Britain it only represented one-seventh of her commerce. In February, Gouverneur Morris approached the French with a request for a loan to equip a fleet; but the response was negative. The news of large-scale British captures of American ships in the Caribbean inflamed public opinion to such an extent that even Hamilton had to go with the tide and press for military preparations. But the object of the Federalists was simply to improve the American bargaining position in order to pave the way for another attempt at a general settlement. A temporary embargo was put on the departure of all shipping from American ports, but this was combined with the nomination of Chief Justice Jay as a special envoy to London. A non-intercourse Bill was defeated in the Senate by Adams's casting vote, and Jay was left to make the best he could of the existing situation.

Again, it was not naval affairs alone which had to be considered in trying to regulate the relations between the United States and Great Britain. The years of Jefferson's retirement, so eventful in Europe, were no less eventful in the remote American west, and fraught there with consequences no less significant for the future of mankind. For the 1790's were not only the decade of the French Revolution: they were also the decade which saw the birth of the American Middle West. The political and social ideas released by the French Revolution and the economic pattern of the modern world's greatest single nucleus of economic power, the Middle West—their interaction is surely the major theme of contemporary history.

As Professor J. B. Brebner points out in his book, *The North Atlantic Triangle*: "While Great Britain and the United States were struggling towards some compromise of their competition in the oceanic carrying trade, substantial layers of the North American population from Georgia to the Canadas were paying very little heed." Congenital restlessness and impatience with difficulties at home, the pressure of European immigration behind them and the growth of their own numbers, made them unable to suspend westward movement. The new settlers were indifferent to politics, and were willing to try their luck under the Spanish flag to the south or the British to the north. The original "loyalists" of Ontario were joined by large numbers of new American migrants who, if they called themselves "loyalists," did so only to qualify for the special land-grants to which they thus became entitled. By 1812, 80 per cent. of the inhabitants of Upper Canada (Ontario) were Americans or their descendants, and only a quarter of these were genuine "loyalists." A further influx of Americans from New England and New York made their way into the lands to the south and east of Montreal.

But even more important was the surge of American settlers into the Ohio valley. The British domination of the country through the retention of the posts, whether justified or not by a desire to keep the peace with the Indians, was intolerable if it meant that the Indians were to stay and the settlers to live under the constant threat of savage border conflicts. The Indians themselves were by no means disposed patiently to await the outcome of Anglo-American diplomacy, in which their interests might only be a bargaining counter. A victory in 1791 over the forces of General St. Clair at a point ninety miles north of the present city of Cincinnati filled them with confidence in their military prowess. An attempt to negotiate a peaceful settlement in 1793 broke down over irreconcilable views as to where the frontier of settlement should run, and not, as was widely thought, owing to British intrigue. This breakdown split the western Indian tribes from the Iroquois, who favoured an agreement with the Americans and forced the former to fight alone. Once this happened, they were bound to rely on being able to fall back on the depleted British garrisons in the forts; the British would at last have to choose between fighting and withdrawal.

The crisis came rapidly. In the autumn of 1793, Anthony Wayne, a hero of the War of Independence, led a small force into the heart of the Indian country and established himself in a fortified post. In February 1795, Lord Dorchester, the governor of Lower Canada, irritated by Genêt's attempts to sow sedition among the French Canadians, made an inflammatory speech which could only be interpreted as a promise that Great Britain would fight. He also ordered the establishment of a British post on the Maumee so as to cover the important post at Detroit. In the spring Wayne advanced to a new position, and the Indians again rejected peace-terms. The frontier-tension was reflected, with the inevitable delays of the time, in acrimonious diplomacy at Philadelphia and London. But Dorchester had no mandate to precipitate war. Wayne's crushing victory over the Indians at the Battle of Fallen Timbers on August 20, 1794, fought within sound of the British fort on the Maumee, did not involve the main body of British troops, although sixty Canadian militiamen had actually joined in the fray. The Americans refrained from attempting to force the British out of their position and the matter was left to diplomacy.

The final British acceptance of American domination in the area, which was involved in the abandonment of the posts, made a renewal of Indian resistance unthinkable. There were now no physical obstacles to settlement. The land policies whose earlier framing had occupied Jefferson during his service in the Continental Congress were consolidated in a new Act of 1796. Land offices were opened at Pittsburgh and Cincinatti. By 1800 the territory of Ohio had a population of 45,000; in 1803 it was admitted into the Union as a state; in 1810 its population was 230,000. "Disease, alcohol and rifles" extinguished the tribes. The dreams of expanding empire were coming true.

Jay's mission to London was thus the meeting-point of many strands in the external and internal politics of his country. Some American historians have stressed the sacrifices made by the Americans in the treaty which their envoy ultimately signed on November 14, 1794. The failure of Jay to get better terms was due, it is said, to the assurances received by the British from Hamilton to the effect that there would be no combination between the United States and other neutrals on the model of the Armed Neutrality of 1780, and to the fact that Jay had been authorized to make concessions on all points for the sake of gaining admittance to the West Indies trade. Others point out that the threat of a general combination of the neutral powers was anyhow an empty one.

It is true that the American position on neutral rights and on impressment was not sustained, although Britain agreed to discuss the question of contraband and of the principle of "free ships, free goods" after the war was over, and meanwhile to pre-empt, and not confiscate, provisions and other goods which the Americans denied were contraband. But commercial relations between the two countries were finally established on a non-discriminatory basis: American ships were to be admitted into the British East Indies and under certain restrictions into the British West Indies. Outstanding financial claims arising out of the War of Independence and the naval spoliations were to be settled through mixed commissions.

More important and more lasting was the effect of the treaty on the American West. The long and complicated dispute over the location of the northwestern boundary of the United States was carried nearer final settlement by the appointment of a joint commission to survey the area. The controversy had arisen as a result of the inadequate geographical knowledge possessed by the framers of the Peace Treaty of 1783, who, among other errors, had put the source of the Mississippi too far to the north, and thus, wrongly, in Canadian territory. The treaty had provided for joint navigation of the Mississippi, and when the error was discovered, the British argued in favour of moving the boundary south, so as to include at least a portion of the river's course. But although Jay's treaty repeated the stipulation for joint navigation of the Mississippi, he refused to admit that this affected the territorial issue. The matter was not finally settled until later, but ultimately a very important part of the Middle West—including the Minnesota iron deposits, which played so vital a rôle in World War II—came under United States instead of Canadian sovereignty; and the final boundary to the Pacific was drawn well to the north of where it would have been if the British proposals had been accepted. Finally, it was the settlement of the other issues which brought Britain to agree to evacuate the northern posts by 1796, thus consolidating for the Americans the fruits of Wayne's victory.

The most recent historian of these events, Professor A. L. Burt, gives full credit to Jay for the success of the negotiations in their primary purpose of avoiding war and for the practical advantages which he secured, and concludes that "by persuading Grenville to accept the joint-commission method as a cure for festering international sores, he (Jay) did more than turn the difficult corner of that day. He ushered in a new era in the history of diplomacy. His treaty inaugurated the modern use of the judicial process in international affairs."

The exact relationship between the conclusion of Jay's treaty and the other major achievement of Federalist diplomacy, Pinckney's treaty with Spain, signed on October 27, 1795, is not clear. But it is obvious that it was the possibility of an Anglo-American rapprochement emphasized in the Mississippi article of Jay's treaty, together with Spain's problems in Europe, which brought the Spaniards to agree to a settlement that in so many respects met the Americans' wishes. The boundary was fixed where they claimed it should be; each side was to refrain from intriguing with the Indians in the territories of the other, and finally the Spaniards and the Americans were to share the whole navigation of the Mississippi, while the Americans were to have a free entrepôt for the transhipment of their goods on its lower reaches—the location of this being fixed for the first three years at New Orleans.

Pinckney's treaty killed all thought of Kentucky separatism, and made the whole West conscious of the importance of its joint interest in its common artery. The Senate ratified the treaty unanimously, although Jefferson, full of party spirit, complained to Madison that it would have "some disagreeable features, seeds of chicanery and eternal broils, instead of peace and friendship."

But the full venom of Republican hostility was reserved for Jay's treaty. "So general a burst of dissatisfaction never before appeared against any transaction," wrote Jefferson when its terms were published: "Those who understand the particular articles of it, condemn these articles. Those who do

163

not, condemn it generally as wearing a hostile face to France." It was, he asserted, "an infamous act," really nothing more than "a treaty of alliance between England and the Anglomen of this country against the people and legislature of the United States."

For the first time, the complicated procedure prescribed by the American Constitution for the ratification of treaties received a full test. The treaty was got through the Senate largely because the Federalists succeeded in having the text kept secret and the debates held in private. Its publication by a member of the minority produced the expected storm. Washington went ahead and signed it, and ratifications were exchanged, although the West Indies clause was omitted, since the Senate had rejected it rather than accept the limitations upon the concession. (The British, in fact, for the sake of their own colonies, gave the Americans the same rights by unilateral action.) The Senate's objection arose partly from the fact that one of the conditions forbade the United States to export certain products of the West Indies, including cotton; but the importance of this commodity was of course unforeseen, as it was only two years since Jefferson, then still Secretary of State, had asked Eli Whitney for more details of the cotton gin that he wished to patent.

The ratification did not end the dispute over the treaty, since the Republicans upheld Jefferson's view that the Senate's action did not commit the House of Representatives. And the Republicans in the latter only failed by three votes to reject the necessary appropriations of money for the joint commissions.

It is difficult to see anything but party feeling in Jefferson's attitude to Jay's treaty; his suspicions of the Anglophil party did not diminish. In May 1797, when already Vice-President, he wrote that the English would not be content with equality, but wanted a monopoly of commerce and influence with the Americans and had in fact obtained it.

"When we take notice that theirs is the workshop to which we go for all we want; that with them centre either immediately or ultimately all the labors of our hands and lands; that to them belongs either openly or secretly the great mass of our navigation; that even the factorage of their affairs here is kept to themselves by factitious citizenships; that these foreign and false citizens now constitute the great body of what are called our merchants, fill our sea-ports, are planted in every little town and district of the country, sway everything in the former places by their own votes and those of their dependents, in the latter by their insinuations and the influence of their ledgers; that they are advancing fast to a monopoly of our banks and public funds, and thereby placing our public finances under their control; that they have in their alliance the most influential characters in and out of office; when they have shewn that by all these bearings on the different branches of the government they can force it to proceed in whatever direction they dictate, and bend the interests of this country entirely to the will of another; when all this, I say, is attended to, it is impossible for us to say that we stand on independent ground, impossible for a free mind not to see and to groan under the bondage in which it is bound."

It is probable that it is in this persistent and long-cherished suspicion of British influence and its supporters that one must seek for the origins of Jefferson's abandonment of his earlier acquiescence in a purely agrarian economy for the United States, and his gradual adoption of a policy of self-sufficiency in all essentials.

In spite of Jefferson's growing concern with politics in 1796, there is no evidence that he actively schemed to return to the national scene, nor any reason to doubt his assertions that the thought of office was unwelcome, or that once Washington's withdrawal was certain, he would welcome the election of John Adams in preference to his own. The two had recently come closer together in their common enmity to Hamilton; indeed, Jefferson seems to have regarded Adams as the only alternative to the election of Hamilton himself. The partisans of Hamilton put up Thomas Pinckney of South Carolina as the other Federalist candidate; (under the Constitution as it then stood, there was a single ballot for both President and Vice-President). The Republican party, still a coalition of heterogeneous geographical and social elements, remained pivoted on the Virginia–New York alliance. This had been exemplified in 1792, when Virginia and North Carolina threw their votes to Clinton rather than Adams. It was now consolidated by the nomination, together with Jefferson, of Aaron Burr of New York.

Washington endeavoured, in his Farewell Address of September 17, 1796, to mitigate the party strife which was certain to break out with redoubled fury when some less respected and less autocratic figure succeeded to the Presidency. The growing tendency of party divisions to be based on sectional alignments was indeed a dangerous one in a federation, and Washington tried instead to picture the Union as one designed by nature for the mutual sustenance of its various regions—an idea which was becoming, as we have seen, less uncongenial to Jefferson's way of thought, and was eventually to find expression in Henry Clay's "American system."

Washington had stressed the harmful internal effect of disputes over foreign policy based on "permanent, inveterate antipathies against particular nations, and passionate attachments for others," and recommended, as the best guarantee of peace and the best safeguard against foreign intervention in American affairs, a policy of "good faith and justice towards all nations."

In phrases which were later to commend themselves to his countrymen as a permanent guide in the conduct of their foreign relations, Washington expressed the essentials of American isolationism:

"The great rule of conduct for us in regard to foreign nations is, in extending our commercial relations, to have with them as little political connection as possible. . . .

"Europe has a set of primary interests, which to us, have none, or a very remote relation. Hence she must be engaged in frequent controversies, the causes of which are essentially foreign to our concerns. Hence, therefore, it must be unwise in us to implicate ourselves, by artificial ties, in the ordinary vicissitudes of her politics, or the ordinary combinations and collisions of her friendships or enmities."

While existing engagements should be scrupulously respected, it was America's true policy "to steer clear of permanent alliances with any portion of the foreign world," and to rely on her growing strength and increasing unity to ensure respect for her neutrality.

But posterity's endorsement of the Farewell Address could not have been guessed at from the indifference of contemporaries to its primary message. "The baneful effects of the spirit of party" were never more obvious than in the election of 1796, and although neither Adams nor Jefferson took part in the fray, the two sides filled the Press with lurid denunciations of their opponents. The veteran statesman of the Revolution and the best representative of the disinterested spirit of public service which his contemporaries inherited from their Puritan past was denounced as a lover of monarchy and aristocracy. Jefferson, Virginian aristocrat and a man interested above all in the practical amelioration of the human condition, was branded as a sans-culotte, an empty theoretician, an atheist and a coward. Radicalism in politics, infidelity in religion and immorality in personal conduct were assumed to go together. On both sides, the reputed bias of the other in foreign affairs was heavily exploited—although Jefferson's views on Jay's treaty make it difficult to repudiate this charge.

By now the original idea of the Founding Fathers that the Presidential electors should exercise their discretion was breaking down, and the voting followed very closely party, which in fact meant sectional, lines. The South and Pennsylvania were for Jefferson; the North and Maryland for Adams. But the divisions in both parties were sufficiently acute for thirty-eight votes to be scattered among four other candidates. In the end, the fact that one elector from each of three Republican states gave his vote to Adams put him by that much ahead of Jefferson; Hamilton's candidate Pinckney was another nine votes behind.

Adams thus took office with the knowledge that his majority in the country was of the narrowest and with his principal rival as his Vice-President. It appeared possible at first that Adams and Jefferson would work together and attempt to steer a middle course, although Jefferson held that his official functions were constitutionally confined to the chairmanship of the Senate. In fact, the cabinet which Adams inherited from Washington, and which took its lead from Hamilton, proved an obstacle to any such collaboration, and the administration continued to act along the traditional lines of Federalist policy.

The conduct of the French Directory made it very difficult to do anything else. Monroe, who had been sent to Paris at the same time as Jay was sent to London, attempted to allay French resentment at the latter's success by private assurances that everything would be altered after Washington's retirement, and was recalled by the rightfully indignant

President. Since Monroe had secured certain allevia-
tions of the French maritime régime before the provisions of Jay's treaty were made public, the French
likewise felt themselves betrayed by the American
envoy who had made public demonstrations of his
enthusiasm for their cause. The Directory now returned to the full rigour of their policy, and declared their intention of retaliating for Jay's treaty
by treating American shipping precisely as did
England. Washington's new envoy was not even
received, and all diplomatic relations between the
United States and France were suspended.

Adams determined upon the expedient of a
special mission such as had brought about treaties
with Great Britain and Spain. But his three envoys
were treated with contempt by the new French
foreign minister, Talleyrand, and were informed
through intermediaries that a prerequisite for any
negotiations would be a bribe for Talleyrand and
his colleagues in corruption, and a loan for France
on terms which meant that it would actually be a
gift. Talleyrand was once more speculating on the
American unwillingness to go to war, and on the
belief that the internal opposition to the Federalists
would paralyse any action Adams might wish to
take—in this he was encouraged by the conduct of
Elbridge Gerry, the Republican member of the
mission, and one of Jefferson's principal confidants
in New England.

The French, however, overplayed their hand.
Adams declared himself unready to send another
envoy to France until assurances had been received
that he would receive the proper respect due to

"the representative of a great, free, powerful and independent nation." Republican opposition to proposals that the country should be put on a war footing was swept aside when the despatches from France proved the soundness of Adams's case, and the necessary Bills rapidly passed through Congress. Commerce with France and its empire was suspended and a limited and undeclared war at sea was begun, although acts which would bring about a formal state of war were avoided. Nevertheless, Washington agreed that, if necessary, he would come out of retirement to lead the American army, provided Hamilton was made second in command. The reappearance of Hamilton seemed to indicate that war would come, and that advantage would be taken of the situation to bring about a closer contact with Great Britain, which had been relaxing its own obstructions to United States commerce. Guns from Charleston harbour, seized during the War of Independence and taken to Halifax, were re-loaned by the British and the loan was turned into a gift.

There is reason to believe that Hamilton was planning for a vast Anglo-American offensive against the French and Spanish dominions in the New World and the summoning of the Spanish colonies to rebellion through Miranda, since Spain was now France's ally once more; on their side the French were planning an attack on Canada, intriguing with Vermont separatists and scheming for a new northern and western dominion in America.

Jefferson himself remained unmoved by the agitation which so powerfully affected the masses of his countrymen. In the summer of 1797 he was hostile to all measures of preparedness, and expressed the view that only the news of French successes and British calamities had prevented the administration from forcing the country into war. He thought that the result of the war spreading to the American continent would be the re-establishment of the French in Louisiana. Then, after the European wars, Louisiana land-grants would be used to pay off the armies of the Republic, and the American West would have a new powerful and populous neighbour.

Although Jefferson professedly deplored the warmth of party feeling and the fact that now for the first time in his experience it was affecting private relations, his letters show a constant concern about the strength of parties. His hopes for the future seemed pinned entirely upon a capture by the party of the entire machinery of government; and every symptom of its advance, particularly outside the South, was the subject of his eager attention. The philosophic statesman was almost concealed for a time beneath the lineaments of the party boss. Yet even when passions were running highest, the longer view was not excluded, as when he called attention more than once to the significance of the negro revolt in San Domingo, which he held provided an unanswerable argument for the emancipation of slaves in the United States while there was yet time. Should the negroes triumph in other West Indian islands, then these might be used for the colonization of the freedmen from the mainland. Meanwhile, Adams's support for the negro insurgents and the exclusion of San Domingo from the prohibition of trade with French dependencies were dangerous for the southern states.

But it was the question of war and peace which dominated all political issues. In the spring of 1798 Jefferson strove to delay a fatal breach with France until the upshot of the projected invasion of England was known. The success of this enterprise would finally eliminate the danger of war.

"The subjugation of England," he wrote, "would indeed be a general calamity. But happily it is impossible. Should it end in her being only republicanized, I know not on what principle a true republican of our country could lament it, whether he considers it as extending the blessings of a purer government to other portions of mankind, or strengthening the cause of liberty in our own country by the influence of that example. I do not indeed wish to see any nation have a form of government forced on them; but if it is to be done, I should rejoice at it being a freer one."

At the beginning of April 1798 he wrote of the importance of delaying war measures so as to gain the summer:

"Time will be given, as well for the public mind to make itself felt as for the operations of France to have their effect in England as well as here. If, on the contrary, war is forced on, the tory interest continues dominant, and to them alone must be left, as they alone desire to ride on the whirlwind and direct the storm. The present period therefore of two or three weeks is the most eventful known since that of 1775, and will decide whether the principles established by that contest are to prevail, or give way to those they subverted."

When the administration released the correspondence of its envoys to France—the X. Y. Z. correspondence as it came to be known after the letters used instead of the names of Talleyrand's emissaries —Jefferson realized that the effect upon the public and upon Congress particularly would be profound. As he interpreted it, the correspondence did not "offer one motive the more" for going to war; the whole thing was a dish "cooked up" by Marshall, who had been one of the envoys. What the French really wanted, he asserted, was a public withdrawal of the hostile expressions used towards them in Adams's strongly worded message to Congress in the previous April. The other demands were only in lieu of this withdrawal, and there was no evidence that Talleyrand was implicated in the demand for a bribe. Jefferson admitted that at the moment "all the passions" were boiling over, and that anyone who kept himself "cool and clear of the contagion" found himself "insulated in every society." The tactics of the peace party were therefore to acquiesce in internal measures of preparedness, but not in any external measures which might act as a provocation to open war. Meanwhile, the heavy weight of taxation which the military proposals required could be relied on to abate the war-fever.

Jefferson tried unsuccessfully to influence the French to act so as to moderate the strength of opinion against them, unwisely giving credentials to a Quaker pacifist and busybody, George Logan, who went to Paris and returned full of assurances of the Directory's peaceful intentions—conduct which led to a special Act of Congress to prevent such unofficial missions. Jefferson also had talks with Victor Du Pont (son of the physiocrat), whom Adams had refused to receive as consul-general.

But at a time when events seemed to be turning against him and his party, Jefferson was presented by Adams with an unexpected opportunity for reversing the political tide. The Administration, fearing war and the internal effects of pro-French propaganda in such an event, managed to secure from Congress a series of measures which involved considerable interference with democratic liberties —measures more stringent in Jefferson's view than those which Pitt had found it necessary to enact in Great Britain.

Four such Acts were passed in June and July 1798. The first extended the term of residence requisite for naturalization from five to fourteen years, the second gave the President the right to expel any alien whose presence he considered dangerous. The third empowered him to expel the nationals of any state with which the United States might be at war or to impose any necessary restraints upon them; and under the last, American citizens could be charged with sedition for a very widely defined range of expressions.

The Federal Government succeeded in securing a number of convictions under the Sedition Act from the fiercely Federalist bench; and the Chief Justice, Oliver Ellsworth, thundered violently against "the French system-mongers, from the quintumvirate at Paris to the Vice-President and minority in Congress . . . apostles of atheism, anarchy, bloodshed and plunder."

The Alien and Sedition Acts produced an immediate reaction in the country, particularly in the Republican South, not only because of their inherent obnoxiousness, but because they assumed for the Federal Government powers which the state regarded as damaging to their own. For almost the first time since the ratification of the Federal Constitution, the question of the rights and powers of the states in relation to the Union raised its head. For Jefferson, whose pro-French reputation was now a handicap, the chance to direct public attention to domestic politics was one to be seized with both hands.

His fears that the Constitution was being stretched so as to provide the Federal Government with new powers had been voiced at the time of the Bank Bill and again in 1796, when Madison suggested that Congress should be allowed to appropriate the post-office surplus to the building of post-roads. Since 1793 the Federal justices had been punishing sedition on the theory that the Federal judiciary had powers deriving from a common law of the United States, the existence of which was denied altogether outside the Federalist party. Now the judges were fortified by legislation, but even so they asserted their right to go beyond the views of Congress in dealing with cases of treason, and to be the final authority for the construction of the Constitution and the laws.

It is difficult to know how serious were Jefferson's suspicions that the Alien and Sedition Acts were "merely an experiment on the American mind, to see how far it will bear an avowed violation of the constitution," and that if they were successfully enforced, the Presidency would be made one for life, and ultimately hereditary, and the office of Senator also a life one. "A least," he said, "this may be the aim of the Oliverians, while Monk and the Cavaliers (who are perhaps the strongest) may be playing their game for the restoration of his most gracious Majesty George the Third." But serious or not, the propagandist value of such suggestion was undeniable.

Jefferson's difficulty was not so much to arouse sentiment as to control it; for there were persons in the South, such as the fiery John Taylor, who thought that redress from the dominantly Federalist East was unobtainable, and that the only remedy was the secession of the southern states, beginning with Virginia and North Carolina. As Jefferson pointed out, no federation could exist if every minority adopted secession as its remedy. The business of a minority was to turn itself into a majority, and to that business the Vice-President set his hand.

For welding together the Republican party on the platform of States Rights, a statement of principles was required, and this was provided in the resolutions which Jefferson framed for the Kentucky legislature and Madison for that of Virginia. These were passed in November and December 1798.

The Kentucky resolutions denied that the Acts objected to were constitutional, and declared that they swept away the barrier of the Constitution "against the passions and the powers of a majority and Congress." But their most striking feature was the statement of a theory of the Constitution which was essentially new. The Resolutions set forth, in comparatively familiar terms, the notion that the Federal Government was the product of a compact between the several states to delegate certain of their powers and no others to a single authority. What was novel was the assertion that the Federal Government was in no way the judge of the extent of these powers, but that "as in all other cases of compact among parties having no common judge, *each party has an equal right to judge for itself, as well as of infractions as of the mode and measure of redress.*" For the moment the only positive suggestion made was that other states should join with Kentucky in petitioning Congress for a repeal of the Acts.

The replies received from other states showed the hardening of the geographical line between parties. In every state north of the Potomac, the state legislatures disapproved of the resolutions, and in most cases adhered to the view that the decision as to the constitutionality of legislation had been entrusted to the Federal Judiciary. The Republican states endorsed the protests and denied the exclusive claim of the Courts to pronounce on the validity of Acts of Congress, without always assenting to the view that it lay with state legislatures to declare them void.

The platform was too good a one lightly to be abandoned, and Madison and Jefferson went on working to give body to their party's constitutional doctrines. Madison did this in the form of a report for the Virginia legislature on the replies received from the other states, and Jefferson employed himself at Philadelphia in seeing that it received wide circulation. The Kentucky legislature passed a second set of resolutions in November 1799. These denied any intention of Kentucky's seceding from the Union, but declared that an acceptance of the right of Congress to define its own powers involved nothing short of despotism. With a boldness of language which may well have exceeded the intent of their framers, the resolutions proclaimed:

"That the several States who formed that instrument [the Constitution] being sovereign and independent, have the unquestionable right to judge of the infraction; and that a nullification by those sovereignties of all unauthorized acts done under color of that instrument is the rightful remedy." Nevertheless, no intention of doing more than protesting could be gleaned either from the declarations or from the actions of the states. Later events, which brought the theory of nullification into prominence, gave an interest to the Kentucky resolutions of a kind which contemporaries could not share. The novelty of their doctrines meant a long delay before they could supplant those of the Federalists. As more than once in Jefferson's career, the occasion produced from him something bigger than itself, and a party manifesto got itself embedded in the portentous documentation of American constitutional history.

The domestic issue of the Alien and Sedition

Acts was the more welcome, since Adams, after having been driven to the brink of war, suddenly decided to act without his colleagues and make another attempt to secure peace. He was fearful that a war would connect the United States too closely with Great Britain, even though alive to the other danger that France might in some way secure the cession to herself of the Floridas and Louisiana and to the strain which this would put upon the loyalty of the western settlers. On their side, the French feared that if war came, the Americans might themselves step in and seize Louisiana, thus putting an end to the reviving French dreams of a New World empire.

In February 1799, Adams nominated William Vans Murray as minister to France. Adams's action met with violent opposition, from the members of his cabinet, which lost him, early in the following year, his Secretary of State and Secretary for War, and from the Federalists in Congress. But the most that the opposition could do was to get two more persons joined with Murray in the commission. By the time the commission arrived in France in March 1800, the "Eighteenth Brumaire" had come and gone, and power in France was in the hands of Napoleon Bonaparte, as First Consul. On September 30, 1800, a Convention with France was signed. Commercial relations on the most-favoured-nation basis were re-established, and the two countries' adherence to their old doctrine about contraband and blockade reaffirmed, although with no obligation on the United States to defend it by arms against Great Britain. The danger of war had been averted for the United States, and Bonaparte had reversed in appearance the policies of his predecessors. But the new shift in French policy had its own explanation. On the day after the signature of the Convention, that is, on October 1, 1800, France and Spain signed the secret treaty of San Idelfonso, by which Spain retroceded Louisiana to France. The object cherished by French diplomacy since Genêt's mission to the United States in 1793 had been achieved.

This fact was of course unknown in the United States, but the Federalists had no difficulty in finding grounds for criticizing a Convention which had failed to settle the question of the validity of the old treaties or the American claims for the damage to their maritime trade. Jefferson's reaction to the first news of the Convention in December 1800 was also unfavourable, since it might embroil the United States with Great Britain. After further negotiation, the Senate finally ratified the Convention in December 1801. This might indeed have led to trouble with Britain at sea; but for the moment there was no prospect of this, since the long Anglo-French struggle seemed to be drawing to a close. Negotiations for peace had begun in March 1801, and preliminaries were signed in October. A definitive treaty, including Spain and Holland, was signed at Amiens on March 27, 1802.

The concluding period of Jefferson's occupancy of the post of Vice-President had been devoted to exploiting the disunion among the Federalists, which Adams's move for peace had finally brought into the open. The hopes of supplanting him that his enemies in the party had cherished were dashed by the death of Washington on December 14, 1799; but the split was unhealed, and in spite of the Federalist successes in the elections of 1798, when the war-crisis was at its height, Adams's ability to secure a second term was very doubtful. Nevertheless, Jefferson left nothing to chance. This meant close attention to the fortunes of the Republicans in all the States, particularly since it was the State legislatures which ordinarily chose the presidential electors. Once again the marshalling of the party forces went on, with Jefferson making every effort to keep well into the background. Now that the tide in France had turned the other way, Jefferson was afraid that the habit of looking to France which he had done so much to inculcate might harm instead of assist the cause of republicanism at home. In his comments on Bonaparte's coup, and on the probability that Bonaparte's executive authority would be a life one, he stressed the fact that the French lacked the experience of, and capacity for, majority rule, which the Americans possessed.

The election of 1800 was in many respects similar to that of 1796. The invective hurled at Jefferson was even fiercer, and in the eastern states a particular feature was the activity of the clergy, who denounced Jefferson as an atheist. Jefferson himself suspected other motives. The Sedition Act had, in his view, broken down the force of the first clause in the Bill of Rights which guaranteed freedom of speech and of the press. Now, he wrote, the clergy hoped that its guarantee of freedom of religion could be circumvented also. The clergy, particularly the Episcopalians and Congregationalists, hoped to see the United States acquire an established church: "They believe that any portion of power confided to me will be exerted in opposition to their schemes; and they believe rightly; for I have sworn upon the altar of god, eternal hostility against every kind of tyranny over the mind of man."

Hamilton's open attack upon the Adams candidature was all that was needed to complete the omens in favour of a Republican success. By this time, party lines had hardened and Jefferson and Burr each got 73 votes against the 65 for Adams and 64 for C. C. Pinckney. The result showed that the Federalists were no longer a national party, but the party of the north-eastern states; and successive elections were to confirm this verdict. The country was now clearly Republican as to majority sentiment, but it had not elected a President. The choice between Jefferson and Burr lay in the House of Representatives, with each state exercising only a single vote. Since the Republican states were evenly divided, this meant that the choice was really in the hands of the minority party. Deadlock continued through thirty-five ballots, and Jefferson began to fear a Federalist plot to make the election ineffective. They would then get the Senate to nominate a temporary President of that House and have power handed over to him, or else pass a Bill granting executive authority to John Jay, who had recently been renominated for the post of Chief Justice, or to John Marshall, who had been Secretary of

State since June. But the Federalists were hardly strong enough for this barefaced violation of the spirit of Constitution; their better chance lay in making some kind of bargain with one or other of the rival Republicans. Jefferson had reported, on January 4, 1801, that Burr was believed to have rejected the Federalist approaches. Now, on February 17, the sixth day of balloting, the vote went in favour of Jefferson. Jefferson himself had informed Monroe two days earlier that many attempts had been made to obtain terms and promises from him, and that he had announced unequivocally his refusal to enter his office with his hands tied by previous promises. On the other hand it is possible that Jefferson's scruples were not shared by some of his political friends. However this may be, it is fairly clear that the Federalists had taken fright at the talk of secession or of a new constitutional convention, if their plans were carried through, and had accepted the advice of Hamilton to allow Jefferson to be elected. Hamilton favoured this course, partly because of his belief that Jefferson was less extreme in his views than had been pictured, more prone to uphold the executive power, and too devoted to his popularity to risk alienating large sections of opinion by his measures, and partly because he cherished a deep, and justified, suspicion of Burr.

Jefferson himself believed that the manner of his election had benefited his party, since the mass of the Federalist voters had supported the view that he should be given the preference which his own party had intended, and that the Congressional leaders of the Federalist party in caballing against him had permanently alienated their followers. Republicanism had become the national creed. The election marked, in Jefferson's view, nothing short of a turning-point in the history of the young Republic. The attempt to twist its constitution into an aristocratic or monarchic pattern had been defeated for good. Those leaders who had "discountenanced all advances in science as dangerous innovations" and had "endeavoured to render philosophy and republicanism terms of reproach, to persuade us that man cannot be governed but by the rod, etc.," had been repudiated. The era of progress and enlightenment had begun. And once again it was the United States which would communicate the revolutionary impulse to the rest of the globe. Two days after his inauguration, Jefferson wrote to the veteran revolutionary statesman, John Dickinson:

"A just and solid republican government maintained here will be a standing monument and example for the aim and imitation of the people of other countries; and I join with you in the hope and belief that they will see, from our example, that a free government is of all others the most energetic; that the enquiry which has been excited among the mass of mankind by our revolution and its consequences, will ameliorate the condition of man over a great portion of the globe."

The comment on such expressions by a modern historian (S. E. Morison), that "a little simplicity more or less cannot be deemed a revolution," was one which neither the vanquished nor the victors would have appreciated. More to the taste of the latter were effusions such as that penned by a Massachusetts physician in his diary on January 1, 1801:

"The nineteenth century begins with a fine clear morning wind at S.W. And the political horizon affords as fair a prospect under the administration of Jefferson and returning intercourse with France and us. With the irresistible propagation of the Rights of Man, the eradication of hierarchy, oppression, superstition and tyranny over the world by means of that soul-improving genius polisher—that palladium of all our rational joys—the printing press—whose value tho' unknown by the vulgar slave cannot be sufficiently appreciated by those who would disdain to fetter the image of God."

Chapter Eight

President : Louisiana Purchase
(1801–1805)

IN any study of Jefferson as the representative
figure of the rising American democracy, the
history of his Presidency must come as an anti-
climax. What is there to show in terms of practical
achievement for all the fuss made on both sides in
the election campaign? It must be admitted, very
little. Although one great constructive accomplish-
ment still lay ahead—the acquisition of Louisiana
and its incorporation in the United States—Jefferson's real work was done when he became President,
and the history of his Presidency consists of little
more than the diplomacy of the period, together
with the beginnings of the long battle between
American democracy and the Supreme Court.

It is not difficult to see why this should be so. The
essential point of the Jeffersonian constitutional
creed was that the Federal Government should
have as little as possible to do with internal matters.
"The true theory of our constitution," he wrote in
August 1800, "is surely the wisest and best, that the
states are independent as to everything within
themselves, and united as to everything respecting
foreign nations. Let the general government be
reduced to foreign concerns only, and let our affairs
be disentangled from those of all other nations,
except as to commerce, which the merchants will

187

manage the better the more they are left free to manage for themselves, and our general government may be reduced to a very simple organization and a very inexpensive one; a few plain duties to be performed by a few servants." To a statesman holding this point of view, the position of President of the United States offered few opportunities for ameliorating, except in a negative way, the lot of his fellow-citizens.

The inaugural ceremonies on March 4, 1801, were designed to emphasize the simplicity of the new republican régime. Nor did the new capital, Washington, to which the Government had removed in the previous summer, offer much scope for pageantry or even for the normal amenities of public life. The execution of the magnificent design for the capital city and its public buildings had scarcely begun; it was still unfinished at the time of Lincoln's inauguration sixty years later.

No passage in Henry Adams's brilliant reconstruction of Jefferson's America is more telling than that in which he depicts the federal capital in 1800:

"The half-finished White House stood in a naked field overlooking the Potomac, with two awkward Department buildings near it, a single row of brick houses and a few isolated dwellings within sight and nothing more; until, across a swamp, a mile and a half away, the shapeless, unfinished Capitol was seen, two wings without a body, ambitious enough in design to make more grotesque the nature of its surroundings. The conception proved that the United States understood the vastness of their task, and were willing to stake something on their faith in it. Never did hermit or saint condemn himself to solitude more consciously than Congress and the Executive in moving the Government from Philadelphia to Washington; the discontented men clustered together in eight or ten boarding-houses as near as possible to the Capitol, and there lived, like a convent of monks, with no other amusement or occupation than that of going from their lodgings to the Chambers and back again. Even private wealth could do little to improve their situation, for there was nothing which wealth could buy; there were in Washington no shops or markets, skilled labor, commerce or people. Public efforts and lavish use of public money could alone make the place tolerable; but Congress doled out funds for this national and personal object with so sparing a hand that their Capitol threatened to crumble in pieces and crush Senate and House under the ruins, long before the building was complete."

In the new Senate chamber erected in this symbolic setting of high hopes and limited resources, Thomas Jefferson, after taking the oath of office before his cousin and enemy, John Marshall, whom Adams had appointed Chief Justice only six weeks earlier, delivered his inaugural address before a small company and in a somewhat inaudible voice. Jefferson's early incapacity as an orator had not been remedied by the passing of time; his messages to Congress were to be sent in writing, partly for this reason and partly to emphasize the contrast between republican and monarchical practice. The Washington-Adams practice of addressing Congress in person was not revived until the days of Woodrow Wilson.

The first inaugural must thus be regarded as a literary composition rather than as a speech. Together with the *Notes on Virginia*, the Declaration of Independence and the Kentucky Resolutions, it forms the major expression of the Jeffersonian creed, and like all Jefferson's political writings, is concerned partly with the affairs of the day and partly with the more general problems of government. It differs from the Declaration and the Kentucky Resolutions in that they had been protests against the actions of those in power, and arguments in favour of resisting these actions. The first inaugural was the work of a man whom a great tide of public feeling had carried into office, who was surrounded in office or shortly would be by his political disciples, the new Secretary of State, his fellow-Virginian, James Madison, and the Genevan-born Albert Gallatin, who became Secretary of the Treasury later in the year and upon whom Jefferson relied to unravel the intricacies of Hamiltonian finance which the President confessed himself unable to master.

Jefferson's intention, as he made clear to his political friends beforehand, was to use the occasion for an attempt to unite the country behind the Republican leaders. In his view the masses of the people had always sympathized with the views of which he had been the leading exponent; the Federalists had used the momentary outburst of anger with France to win many Republicans over; now they were back in the fold and should be kept there. The Federalist generals were to be left without an army to lead.

In his speech he affirmed his belief that now that the issue had been decided, the minority would accept the decision with good grace, confident that the majority would not use their powers for purposes of oppression. "Every difference of opinion is not a difference of principle. We have called by different names brethren of the same principle. We are all Republicans, we are all Federalists." It was wrong to suggest that a Republican Government could not be strong enough to preserve itself. "Sometimes it is said that man cannot be trusted with the government of himself," declared Jefferson, perhaps with John Adams in mind; for his embittered predecessor had left Washington rather than be present at his successor's inauguration—a gesture which his son, John Quincy Adams, repeated when Andrew Jackson defeated him in 1828. "Can he, then, be trusted with the government of others? Or have we found angels in the form of kings to govern him? Let history answer this question."

And then followed a paragraph which may be regarded as the quintessence of the Jeffersonian creed:

"Let us, then, with courage and confidence pursue our own Federal and Republican principles, our attachment to union and representative government. Kindly separated by nature and a wide ocean from the exterminating havoc of one quarter of the globe; too high-minded to endure the degradations of the others; possessing a chosen country, with room enough for our descendents to the thousandth and thousandth generation; entertaining a due sense of our equal right to the use of our own faculties, to the acquisitions of our own industry, to honor and confidence from our fellow-citizens, resulting not from birth but from our actions and their sense of them; enlightened by a benign religion, professed indeed, and practiced in various forms, yet all of them inculcating honesty, truth, temperance, gratitude, and the love of man; acknowledging and adoring an overruling Providence, which by all its dispensations proves that it delights in the happiness of man here and his greater happiness hereafter—with all these blessings, what more is necessary to make us a happy and prosperous people? Still one thing more, fellow-citizens—a wise and frugal Government, which shall restrain men from injuring one another, shall leave them otherwise free to regulate their own pursuits of industry and improvement, and shall not take from the mouth of labor the bread it has earned. This is the sum of good government, and this is necessary to close the circle of our felicities."

The charge of hypocrisy which some contemporaries brought against Jefferson may be held to lie against the allusion here to Providence and to the life hereafter. As Dr. Koch has pointed out with reference to another passage in his writings, "It is difficult to determine whether Jefferson approved the argument of immortality only as an extra incentive to moral behaviour, a kind of Benthamite 'religious sanction,' but without literal or ascertainable truth value, or whether he actually believed in its promise." There is, however, nothing in the inaugural incompatible with his statements in private; and the notion of Providence as here phrased was no bar to Jefferson's settled anticlericalism.

The essential principles of this "wise and frugal" Government were slightly elaborated in another passage which may be taken as the manifesto of the Virginia wing of the Republican party, although as Henry Adams pointed out, the wholly negative temper of the Virginia creed was not altogether suited to the imaginative and enterprising mind of Jefferson "who represented the hopes of science as well as the prejudices of Virginia," nor very appealing to the northern democrats who were an essential component of the party:

"Equal and exact justice to all men, of whatever state or persuasion, religious or political; peace, commerce, and honest friendship with all nations, entangling alliances with none; [a phrase too often attributed to Washington!] the support of the State governments in all their rights, as the most competent administrations for our domestic concerns and the surest bulwarks against anti-republican tendencies; the preservation of the General Government in its whole constitutional vigor [a reassurance to the Federalists], as the sheet anchor of our peace at home and safety abroad; a jealous care of the right of election by the people—a mild and safe corrective of abuses which are lopped by the sword of revolution where peaceable remedies are unprovided; absolute acquiescence in the decisions of the majority, the vital principle of republics, from which is no appeal but to force, the vital principle and immediate parent of despotism; a well-disciplined militia, our best reliance in peace and for the first moments of war till regulars may relieve them; the supremacy of the civil over the military authority; economy in the public expense, that labor may be lightly burthened; the honest payment of our debts and sacred preservation of the public faith; encouragement of agriculture and of commerce as its handmaid; the diffusion of information and arraignment of all abuses at the bar of the public reason; freedom of religion; freedom of the press, and freedom of person under the protection of the habeas corpus and trial by juries impartially selected."

When Jefferson came to elaborate upon these general ideas and to turn them into a programme of action, it was obvious that, as far as the Federal Government was concerned, the only thing called for was the reduction of expenditure, and the lightening of the burden of taxation. This was largely done through reducing the navy and replacing ocean-going frigates with coastal gunboats. But even though the Great Powers were at peace, and the question of protecting American commerce not an urgent one, the Americans were by this time engaged in a war which the ruler of Tripoli had declared upon them. This war went on in desultory fashion until 1805, when Jefferson, previously so strong an adherent of the use of force against the Barbary pirates, made peace upon terms which were not very glorious, and withdrew American shipping from the Mediterranean.

The legislative activity of the first two years of Jefferson's Presidency was of little importance, except for two measures which strengthened both the Government and the party: the admission of Ohio as a state, and the acquisition from Georgia by the Federal Government of her claims to the lands which were later to become the states of Mississippi (1817) and Alabama (1819). In the north-west, the tide of immigration was spilling over from Ohio into Indiana; in the south-west, the demand for cotton would soon spread the plantation system far beyond the boundaries of the seaboard states of the old South. The sectional conflict which produced the Civil War was dimly prefigured; but for the moment the West was a single force, and one which played an ever-increasing rôle in directing the fortunes of the American democracy.

From the point of view of the active politician, the crucial question as always was one of jobs—whom would Jefferson appoint to office? It rapidly became clear that the phrase, "we are all Republicans, we are all Federalists," was not meant to apply here. Adams had used the period between his defeat and Jefferson's assumption of office to fill as many offices as possible with his own supporters; it would not have been human for Jefferson to accept the situation, and his followers would hardly have permitted it. "Jefferson," wrote Henry Adams, "resembled all rulers in one peculiarity of mind. Even Bonaparte thought that a respectable minority might be useful as censors; but neither Bonaparte nor Jefferson was willing to agree that any particular minority was respectable." Where the law permitted removals, the Federalists would have to go, and their offices be awarded to deserving Republicans, or used as patronage with which to build up the party in the areas where it was weakest. For Jefferson had no desire to see the Federalists retreat unmolested to some New England Byzantium. "To the victors belong the spoils"—as so often in politics, the practice preceded the theory.

There was one department of national life where Executive discretion was not unhampered. The Federal Judiciary was organized under statute and its appointments were for life. The Judiciary Act of 1801 had enlarged the structure set up under the original Act of 1789, mainly by creating a new class of circuit justices in addition to the justices of the Supreme Court; and this had been done, in Jefferson's view, in order to have as many posts as possible to fill up with Federalists. So long as the Federal Judiciary, manned by Federalists and claiming the last word on constitutional matters, was intact, there would, he believed, be a perpetual danger of centralization and of the state courts and state governments losing their proper authority. The issue was a dangerous one, because although the Virginians were ready to rally to the call of States Rights, the northern Republicans were less ready to attack the judiciary directly; Aaron Burr, the Vice-President, not only for this reason, soon became disaffected to the party's leadership. Jefferson was then forced to intervene in the murky depths of New York's internal politics. The philosopher in politics is always well advised to remain in opposition—and Jefferson was not at his best in the struggle with the Supreme Court and John Marshall.

Apart from the political, personal and party undercurrents, the question of the judiciary had a deep significance for the future of American democracy. One strong trend in the thought of Jefferson and his associates was concerned with the protection of individuals and minorities against legislative or executive oppression. For this purpose there could be no better bulwark than an independent judiciary. On the other hand, the Supreme Court had upheld Adams's obnoxious Sedition Act, and by its tendency to recognize a federal common law had itself become an engine of consolidation. The other strong trend in Jeffersonian political theory was respect for majority rule; here the Court, by permitting appeals from the state courts, and calling into question the constitutionality of state legislation, was defying popular majorities. The dilemma was inescapable, and the solution of approving the interpretative functions of state courts, while denying those of the federal courts, was neither logical nor convincing.

The immediate question in 1802 was to decide what should be done about Adams's Judiciary Act and whether or not to override the argument that the new judgeships could not be abolished, because if this were done, the life-tenure of their holders would unconstitutionally be set aside.

The debates on the repeal measure ranged far and wide over the whole question of the judiciary —the Federalists upholding its powers of reviewing both state and congressional legislation, the

Republicans taking the view that the will of the people as expressed by their representatives must prevail. So far indeed had the reversal of rôles between the two parties now gone, that the Federalists —a regional minority group—were now employing the threats of the Virginia secessionists and the doctrines of the Kentucky resolutions.

Although the Act of 1801 was duly repealed by the triumphant Republicans, they did not do more than re-establish the organization of the Court as it stood in 1789; its jurisdiction was unaffected and the extent of its powers still undetermined.

The real crisis came in 1803. To some extent it was the Court, that is to say, John Marshall, rather than the Republican party that precipitated it. Some of Marshall's associates were old and feeble, and he feared that in the event of their death or resignation, Jefferson would be able to fill the vacancies with Republicans who would sacrifice the claims of the Court. An opportunity to assert the rights of the Court before this happened arose in the case known as *Marbury v. Madison*. Madison had refused to issue some of the commissions to office, which Adams had signed in the last hours of his Presidency. Marbury, who was to have been made a justice of the District of Columbia, asked the Court for a writ of *mandamus* to the Secretary of State, to compel him to hand over the document. It was known that if judgment were given in Marbury's favour, the Republicans in Congress would impeach Marshall and that Marshall's removal would enable Jefferson to appoint, as Chief Justice, Spencer Roane, Chief Justice of Virginia, an extreme upholder of the States Rights doctrine. On the other hand, if Marshall gave way, it would mean abandoning all legal checks upon the Executive.

Marshall's solution to the dilemma has been called by his admiring biographer, Senator A. J. Beveridge, "a coup as bold in design and daring in execution, as that by which the Constitution had been framed." In brief, Marshall accepted Marbury's claim that the commission had been wrongfully detained by Madison, but denied the Supreme Court's ability to act, on the ground that the section of the Judiciary Act of 1789 giving it the power of issuing writs of *mandamus* was unauthorized by the provisions of the Constitution relating to the orginal jurisdiction of the Court. In thus invalidating an Act of Congress for the first time, Marshall followed reasoning which was very close to that Hamilton had employed in the *Federalist*.

The power of invalidating legislative Acts arose, in his view, from the very fact of the existence of a written Constitution, assigning specific and definite duties and rights to the separate organs of government. If "the courts are to regard the constitution and the constitution is superior to any ordinary act of the legislature, the constitution and not such an ordinary act must govern the case to which they both apply." The fact that it was an Act of Congress which had been invalidated was, as it happens, a comparatively minor one from the political point of view, since it was not until fifty-four years had passed that the Court invalidated another. But, as the Republicans saw, the argument

199

would apply equally well to state laws which might come before the Court on appeal. The claim that a nominated body should have not merely a co-ordinate, but a final, decision on what was, or was not, constitutional, was one which could not commend itself to Jefferson's followers—at least not so long as the legislative and executive branches of government were in their hands.

Had Marshall followed up his decision in *Marbury v. Madison* by disallowing the Repeal Act of 1802, the challenge might have been taken up. As it was, the Republicans got themselves tangled up in two impeachments of comparatively minor figures on the federal bench; and the failure of the second of these brought the first assault on the judiciary to an end at the beginning of 1805. The most notable feature of the impeachment proceedings had been the Republican contention that impeachment was a method of removal and not a criminal proceeding; it was obvious that what they were seeking was some way of getting round the permanency of tenure enjoyed by the judges, and of making them responsive to movements in popular opinion. In the arguments of the time can be seen the seeds of the great clash between a Jeffersonian President—Franklin D. Roosevelt—and the Supreme Court in 1936–7.

As President, Jefferson was not directly involved in the party conflict which ranged round the Supreme Court. The age of legislative projects prepared in the White House had not yet dawned, although Jefferson took an active part in seeing that congressional leadership was kept in the right hands. Finance and administration could be left in the charge of the talented Gallatin; Jefferson could employ himself on the proper task of the federal executive—foreign affairs.

The intricate diplomacy of the Louisiana purchase is a story in itself and one which does Jefferson credit. All that can be said here is that the credit was due to him, not so much for far-sighted planning, as for the rapid use of a propitious moment. For the omens had not at first seemed too favourable. That France had designs on Louisiana and the Floridas was known, that some if not all of the territory had been ceded to her by Spain was suspected, whether the United States could prevent this happening was by no means certain. The rôle of a weak neutral between two powerful rivals whether their conflict is on land or sea is not an enviable one. When they fight, the interests of the would-be neutral are certain to be disregarded; when they make peace, it may be at the neutral's expense. At first it seemed as though, after its long battle for maritime rights against France—in which it had been helped by the enforced absence of the French fleet from Caribbean waters—the United States was going to pay for the reconciliation of the Peace of Amiens. For the British seemed prepared to allow Bonaparte to occupy himself with trans-atlantic affairs in preference to matters nearer home; and if he could reduce San Domingo to obedience, he would need to acquire a mainland source of supply in order to build up a new balanced mercantile empire in the west. If this happened soon, the Americans would lose the long-run advantage which the rapid growth of their western settlements was giving them. It was true that the British themselves might intervene if the French went too far; but the British would be still less palatable neighbours than the French. And finally, besides the Great Powers, there was the opposition at home. For although the Federalists had always disliked and feared the westward extension of the Union, the opportunity of winning over followers from the Republican camp would be too good a one to miss, if Jefferson neglected the interests of the western settlements and failed to preserve unimpaired their Mississippi lifeline. Jefferson was aware that the American view by which "Louisiana" lay wholly to the west of the Mississippi had not been readily accepted in Europe; the conduct of all the Great Powers in 1782–3 had shown that they held that the United States ought to stop at the Appalachians. That idea was not dead yet.

For a country which had little military or naval strength, and which was engaged in cutting down such strength as it had, the position was not a strong one, although Jefferson pinned something to the hope that the commercial value of United States' friendship would have some influence. The only solution was to temporize, and even this might end badly. And any policy was difficult to pursue, since the Americans were uncertain of the nature of the Franco–Spanish arrangement, and had to carry on separate negotiations at London and Paris which were hard to co-ordinate from distant Washington. The realization of what was at stake only gradually dawned on Jefferson, whose mind ran on consolidating the settlement of the lands east of the Mississippi and on fusing the Indian population there with the general body of settlers, while, by the Lewis and Clark expedition, first proposed to Congress at the beginning of 1803, the Missouri country was to be opened up as a new fur-trading domain.

But the imaginative was not allowed to cloud the practical. The interests of the United States had to be protected against Bonaparte's designs. For this purpose, Jefferson could rely upon the support of some influential figures in France who sympathized with the view that the whole North American Continent should fall under the republican domain of the United States; and it was through one of these figures, Du Pont de Nemours, who had for three years been living in the United States, that Jefferson made his first overt move to parry the coming blow. He sent Du Pont a letter to take with him to France when he left for that country in April 1802, and also made him the bearer of an open letter to his representative in Paris, Robert Livingston.

In his letter to Dupont de Nemours, Jefferson wrote:

"I wish you to be possessed of the subject, because you may be able to impress upon the government of France, the inevitable consequences of their taking possession of Louisiana; and though as I here mention, the cession of New Orleans and the Floridas to us would be a palliation, yet I believe it would be no more, and that this measure will cost France, and perhaps not very long hence, a war which will annihilate her on the ocean, and place that element

203

under the despotism of two nations which I am not reconciled to the more because my own would be one of them."

To Livingston, Jefferson was even more explicit:

"There is on the globe one single spot, the possessor of which is our natural and habitual enemy. It is New Orleans, through which the produce of three-eighths of our territory must pass to market and from its fertility will ere long yield more than half of our whole produce. France placing herself in that door assumes to us the attitude of defiance. Spain might have retained it quietly for years . . . the day that France takes possession of New Orleans, fixes the sentence which is to restrain her forever within her low water-mark. It seals the Union of two nations, who, in conjunction, can maintain exclusive possession of the ocean. From that moment, we must marry ourselves to the British fleet and nation."

Du Pont, a Frenchman as well as a friend of America, could see the difficulties involved in the scarcely veiled threats of the American approach, and tried to demonstrate the greater dangers which a British alliance would involve. If the Americans could not be satisfied with assurances for the freedom of navigation down the Mississippi, then the best method was for the United States to offer to buy France's claims from her. The latter solution was certainly not ruled out by Madison, but Jefferson took a more bellicose tone and was apparently unwilling to pay for what he had already defined as a natural right.

The very cautious approaches to France in the

early months of 1802 took on a new urgency when it became known that, on October 20, five days after the King of Spain's final order to transfer Louisiana to France, the Spanish intendant at New Orleans had put an end to the American exercise of their rights at that port under the treaty of 1795. Would France be likely to restore what Spain had removed, and possibly removed in agreement with her? At the same time, it was fairly clear that France was pressing on with further plans for the exchange of European against American territory which would have the effect of giving her the Floridas as well—or at least such part of them as had not been included in the transfer of Louisiana. This would mean a total exclusion of the United States from the gulf coast. Tempers rose in Congress, and the Federalists looked like gaining adherents by espousing the war-fever of the West.

While Livingston in Paris spun out his arguments that France could not gain from driving America into British arms and that her purposes did not require the whole of Louisiana and the Floridas, Jefferson had to act. At this juncture there arrived from Du Pont another letter suggesting a treaty for the purchase of New Orleans and the two Floridas. Congress appropriated two million dollars for a special mission to France, and joined James Monroe with Livingston for the purpose. If the commissioners failed to get the minimum required to secure a proper outlet to the Gulf, they were to proceed to London and try to secure a British alliance.

When Monroe left the United States on March 8,

1803, there was no reason to believe that success would be easy, but when he arrived in Paris on April 13, the whole situation had changed. The difficulties in the way of Bonaparte's American project had multiplied: yellow-fever in San Domingo; ice in the Dutch ports where the French Army transports lay; and in the spring of 1803, the general realization that the Peace of Amiens had been only a truce and that war was on the way. It was clear that if war came, the British would seize New Orleans themselves, and possibly secure a firm American alliance as its price.

These facts brought about a swift change of plan on Bonaparte's side. Since the project of an American empire would have to be abandoned, what would the Americans give for the whole of Louisiana? By the time Monroe arrived, negotiations were under way. The treaties which transferred France's claim to Louisiana in return for sixty million francs together with the twenty million francs which U.S. citizens still claimed from France for maritime seizures, were concluded on April 30, 1803. On May 15 Great Britain declared war on France; but Alexander Baring the banker was allowed to travel to Paris and the United States in order to see the financing of this extraordinary transaction—Great Britain did not want to risk anything going wrong.

Although Jefferson's envoys secured more than he had thought possible, this does not mean that he regarded the possession of New Orleans and the guarantee of the Mississippi navigation as an end in itself. The Americans were destined to expand and multiply: the only question was one of timing.

In November 1801, Jefferson wrote to Monroe:

"However our present interests may restrain us within our own limits, it is impossible not to look forward to distant times, when our rapid multiplication will expand itself beyond those limits, and cover the whole northern, if not the southern, continent, with a people speaking the same language, governed in similar forms and by similar laws; nor can we contemplate with satisfaction either blot or mixture on that surface."

For the moment he would be content with what his envoys had gained. Writing to Du Pont in November 1803, he said:

"Our policy will be to form New Orleans and the country on both sides of it on the gulf of Mexico, into a State; and as to all above that, to transplant our Indians into it, constituting them a Maréchaussée to prevent emigrants crossing the river, until we have filled up all the vacant country on this side. This will secure both Spain and us as to the mines of Mexico for half a century, and we may safely trust the provisions for that time to the men who shall live in it."

But as France and Britain became interlocked in their struggle in Europe, Jefferson's ambitions increased. The Louisiana cession was now expanded in Jefferson's mind to include Texas and West Florida as well as a huge undefined area in the North-west. The process of ousting Spanish jurisdiction and British influence from the Floridas began—a process which was to be ratified by the Adams-Onis treaty of 1819. Lewis and Clark set out upon their expedition, and in 1805 reached the mouth of the Columbia River. Britain was in no condition to resist American claims. In May 1803, Rufus King had concluded a convention in London settling the issues outstanding since Jay's treaty, and including a boundary line which duly gave Great Britain access to the Mississippi. But now that the Americans had no rivals on its lower reaches, the British claim to share its navigation was no longer a useful card; and in the course of its passage through the Senate, the Republicans saw to it that this clause disappeared. When the U.S.–Canadian boundary was fixed in the Convention of 1818, the boundary ran north of the headwaters of the Mississippi.

With the growth of Jefferson's expansionist projects, the idea of only gradually permitting the new lands to acquire population was thrown overboard. The interests of the Indians would have to follow into oblivion those of the European rivals for empire. The tide of settlement and of Jeffersonian democracy swept on into the West. As Arthur Burr Darling, an historian of these events, writes: "This was hard. It was ruthless. But it was true to the character of this people."

In securing for the Americans access to the whole interior of the continent Jefferson was expressing the wishes of what was becoming the dominant strain in the United States. But there were obstacles which had to be considered. Jefferson himself was uneasy about the constitutional propriety of his action. The acquisition of territory by the Federal Government might be swallowed; but the treaty had specifically promised that the new lands and their inhabitants should enjoy the full blessings of incorporation into the American Union. Was the Federal Government entitled to do this? Would it not set a new precedent for a latitudinarian construction of the constitution more far-reaching than anything for which the Virginians had attacked Hamilton? Had the international situation in the summer of 1803 been less fluid, Jefferson might have given way to these doubts. But time was important; Bonaparte might regret his decision; so ratification was hurried through in the ordinary way.

For the Federalists of the Eastern States this was a blow indeed. However much they may have wished to use discontent in the West to align the United States with Great Britain against France, a further westward expansion was the last thing they desired. Ever since the negotiations which led to the Peace of 1783, they had striven to prevent the subordination of the eastern seaboard to the uncontrollable democracy of the West. Too few in numbers to vote the project down, the Federalists talked of secession, of the inevitable scission of the Union along the line of the mountains. Jefferson could afford to ignore their spleen. As he told Joseph Priestley, in a letter in January 1804:

"I confess I look to this duplication of area for the extending of a government so free and economical as ours, as a great achievement to the mass of happiness which is to ensue. Whether we remain in one confederacy, or form into Atlantic and Mississippi confederacies, I believe not very important to the happiness of either part. Those of the western confederacy will be as much our children and descendants as those of the eastern, and I feel myself as much identified with that country in future time, as with this; and did I now foresee a separation at some future day, yet I should feel the duty and desire to promote the western interests as zealously as the eastern, doing all the good for both portions of our future family which should fall within my power."

Certainly the immediate political prospect gave some excuse for complacency. After the Louisiana treaty was ratified, the Federalist irreconcilables planned to secure the election of Burr—now totally estranged from Jefferson—to the governorship of New York. Then, with his aid, New York and New Jersey might be swung into line with the New England states to form an independent confederacy. But the plan for a coalition of Federalists and Republican dissidents found no favour with the responsible leaders of federalism, Rufus King and Alexander Hamilton, and for the moment seemed to have no sequel.

On February 25, 1804, the party congressional caucus nominated Jefferson for a second term as President. By this time the twelfth amendment had become law and the Vice-Presidency was a separate matter. Burr was ruled out, and his New York rival, George Clinton, was nominated in his stead. In April Jefferson lost his younger daughter, and the grief of this event overclouded the triumphs of the year. In July a more public tragedy occurred when Burr avenged on Hamilton in a fatal duel the long thwarting of his ambitions. The links with the past were being severed by death, and Jefferson again talked as though he would welcome withdrawal from the public eye. But nothing could prevent his re-election, and in comparison with the bitter conflicts of 1796 and 1800, the campaign was a quiet one. Only two of the (now) seventeen states, Connecticut and Delaware, voted for the Federalists, C. C. Pinckney and Rufus King. Jefferson's vindication was complete.

211

Chapter Nine
President : Embargo
(1805–1809)

AT the beginning of his second term of office in
1805, Jefferson was at the height of his power
and popularity. If the informality of his dress and
manner might offend foreign diplomats, and his
friendship with Thomas Paine and other evidences
of radical thought might be too much for the
upper crust of New England society, the support
of public opinion at large could not be gainsaid;
and the man who had doubled the size of the national domain without the firing of a shot might
well expect the plaudits of a country in which expansionism and pacifism were so often found in
unexpected alliance.

In a letter in the previous December, he
had voiced his self-satisfaction in no uncertain
terms:

"The new century opened itself by committing
us on a boisterous ocean; but all is now subsiding;
peace is smoothing our path at home and abroad;
and if we are not wanting in the practice of justice
and moderation, our tranquillity and prosperity
may be preserved until increasing numbers shall
leave us nothing to fear from abroad. With England
we are in cordial friendship; with France in the
most perfect understanding; with Spain we shall
always be bickering, but never at war till we seek

it. Other nations view our course with respect and friendly anxiety."

Yet the record of Jefferson's second term of office, both at home and abroad, is one of almost unmitigated failure and disappointment. At home the unity which only a weakened Federalist minority seemed to challenge was broken up by new sectional and party rivalries, and these were embittered by the fact that Jefferson early let it be known that he would emulate Washington by refusing a third term, thus provoking an immediate contest for the succession between Madison and Monroe.

But it would be wrong to see no more than the clash of personalities in the struggle which Jefferson had to undertake in order to maintain even a semblance of unity and discipline within the ranks of his own party. Like every succeeding American party with claims to a national following, the Jeffersonian Republicans were in fact a coalition. The closer they got to total victory—and Jefferson's aim was the complete annihilation of the Federalists—the harder it was for the coalition to keep its ranks intact.

The purely negative attitude to the Federal Government which had sufficed in the South for a political theory and which was still represented in Congress by Jefferson's and Madison's principal critic, John Randolph, was hardly suited to a country that now possessed a large territorial empire which it was essential for reasons of defence to open up and settle at the first opportunity. F. J. Turner, the pioneer historian of the American "frontier," has pointed out that the Louisiana purchase was "perhaps the constitutional turning-point in the history of the Republic." It provided a new area for national legislation; and forced the Federal Government to undertake wider responsibilities.

America's growing commerce also provided new problems. Unless undertaken in willing subservience to the dominant sea-power—and after Trafalgar this could only mean Great Britain—it would require naval protection; and expenditure on the navy was the mark of Federalist politics. The watchword of the Republican party was "economy." There was another factor. Buoyant trade meant a rising revenue. While there were still debts to pay, the revenue could be used for debt redemption. But under Gallatin's careful stewardship, the debt was disappearing and a surplus was in prospect. For Jefferson, and for many of his supporters in the Middle States and the West, a surplus of revenue was something to be welcomed rather than feared, and his Second Inaugural Address (March 4, 1805) shows Jefferson in a mood of constructive optimism. Once the redemption of debt has been completed, declares Jefferson,

"the revenue thereby liberated may, by a just repartition of it among the States and a corresponding amendment of the Constitution, be applied *in time of peace* to rivers, canals, roads, arts, manufactures, education, and other great objects within each State. *In time of war,* if injustice by ourselves and others must sometimes produce war, increased as the same revenue will be by increased population and consumption, and aided by other resources reserved for that crisis, it may meet within the year all the expenses of the year without encroaching on the rights of future generations, by burdening them with the debts of the past. War will then be but a suspension of useful works and a return to a state of peace, a return to the progress of improvement."

Internal improvements and a war chest!—even the admission that a constitutional amendment would be required to legitimize the former was hardly consolation to the strict Republicans. But the aloof and reserved Jefferson, never expansive outside the circle of his intimates, was hardly likely to be deterred by possible opposition. In fact, there was no opportunity to try the temper of the country, since foreign affairs soon overshadowed all prospects of domestic improvement; but the fate of similar proposals at a later period suggests that in speaking in this vein, Jefferson was as yet only the spokesman of a minority.

If the question of the powers of the National Government and allied topics were to become reasons for divergence between East and West, it was obvious that the institution of slavery was a source of division between the slave-state Republicans and the party in other sections. The process by which slavery was being more firmly grafted than ever before on to the southern economy, as cotton cultivation grew in importance, was too insidious for contemporaries to fathom as easily as later historians. But it was obvious that the slavery question was very much to the forefront of the southern mind. The Bill for ending the slave trade in 1808— the earliest year by which it was constitutionally feasible—although generally acceptable in principle, showed up sharp divergences between the sections on points of detail. When, in 1806, the commerce with the rebels of San Domingo was forbidden in agreement with Napoleon, the measure received support from southern Republicans, who were otherwise hostile to the alleged subservience of Madison to France. If a free negro republic survived in the Caribbean, they feared for the stability of the South.

Besides the awkward clashes inside the party and the revival of Federalism in New England after its apparent extinction in 1804, there remained the contest with John Marshall and the Supreme Court. The Burr conspiracy and trial which gave Marshall his next opportunity of defying the President was the more galling, in that it is impossible to absolve Jefferson himself from some responsibility for the events which led up to it.

More than one historian has suggested that Jefferson never understood the fortuitous set of favourable circumstances which made the Louisiana purchase possible. Certainly the conduct he pursued with regard to Florida in the early months of his second administration was hardly likely to raise him in the esteem of foreign Powers. For the transparent attempt to bribe or bully Spain into giving up the coveted province, and the vague overtures for a British alliance without any idea of reciprocal support, were unlikely to be taken seriously in a world once more at war. The only justification for such a policy would have been a determination to fight if his demands were not granted; but for fighting Jefferson had neither the heart nor—given the

congressional policy of retrenchment—the resources. So in December 1805, after having talked
as though war were imminent, he abruptly reversed his policy, and tried to buy Florida from
Spain with Talleyrand as his intermediary. The
motives which led Napoleon to play with this
scheme are obscure; but they were certainly French
and not American, and since other events had made
co-operation with Great Britain out of the question,
Napoleon had few motives for conciliating Jefferson.
The fact that the persistent Venezuelan rebel
Miranda was allowed to fit out in New York a fili-
bustering campaign directed against the Spanish
colonies, did not commend the American approaches
to Spain. By the middle of 1806 Napoleon had
formed other plans for Spain and her possessions,
and the United States was no nearer acquiring
Florida and Texas.

It is not surprising that during this equivocal
period in American-Spanish relations, when the
possession of New Orleans was likely to be more of
a liability than an asset in the event of war, the
future of the West should have seemed something
which could at any moment be altered by the action
of a few resolute or merely unscrupulous men. Burr
was to show that he belonged rather to the latter
than the former category. There is no satisfactory
way of accounting for his motives any more than of
defining his objectives. Certainly Burr had little to
complain of Jefferson, who had received him without hostility after he killed Hamilton, and appointed some of his friends to important places in
the administration. Even if, as has been asserted,

217

Jefferson needed Burr to preside over the impeachment of Justice Chase, the fact of his cordiality is undisputed. Clearly, this was insufficient; and during the year 1805 Burr started weaving the strands of a conspiracy so intricate that it has not been altogether unravelled to this day.

As disclosed to loyal Americans, Burr's object was the conquest of Texas and Mexico. And if it seemed odd that this should be a private project, the fact that war with Spain was, on the face of things, so likely made it seem a mere anticipation of national policy—the sort of thing which had happened before in the West. In his contacts with the British, however, the Burr plot took on a darker side, as it suggested the detaching of the western states from the Union and the creating out of these, and out of what could be grabbed from Spain, of a new Confederacy or Empire in close alliance with Great Britain. When hope of British support faded, Burr put a similar scheme, with suitable modifications, before the Spaniards themselves. In view of these extravagant and fantastic imaginings, it is perhaps not surprising that Jefferson failed to take seriously the warnings which reached him about Burr's intrigues. It is all of a piece with the rest of the story that the man who finally brought about Burr's denunciation and arrest was his fellow-conspirator, the senior American general, James Wilkinson, who had himself for twenty years been earning a salary as a secret agent of the King of Spain.

Once the conspiracy was exploded and it became clear that there was no real danger, apart from the general dissatisfaction of the New Orleans creoles with American rule, the question as to how seriously to treat Burr was a difficult one to answer. By this time, Jefferson had come round to the view that it was a very serious matter indeed. In December 1806, before hearing that Burr had fled, Jefferson wrote: "Our Catiline is at the head of an armed body; and his object is to seize New Orleans, from there attack Mexico, place himself on the throne of the Montezumas, add Louisiana to his empire and the Western States from the Alleghany if he can." After Burr had been captured, the whole weight of the Administration was thrown into trying to get a conviction against him.

The trial was held by Marshall sitting as a circuit court judge, with John Randolph as foreman of the jury, and was rapidly turned into an attack on the President through his chief witness Wilkinson. Marshall even went so far as to subpoena Jefferson himself. The fact that Jefferson refused to obey did not strengthen the Administration's case. In the end, by ruling that the testimony provided for by the Constitution in cases of treason had not been furnished, Marshall forced the prosecution to drop the case. Marshall had won another round.

Before the case ended, Jefferson had been infuriated by the way in which the Federalists made "Burr's cause their own."

"If there had been an instance," he wrote on April 20, 1807, "in this or the preceding administrations, of federal judges so applying principles of law as to condemn a federal or acquit a republican offender, I should have judged them in the present case with more charity. All this, however, will work

219

well. The nation will judge both the offender and judges for themselves. If a member of the Executive or Legislature does wrong, the day is never far distant when the people will remove him. They will then see and amend the error in our Constitution which makes any branch independent of the rest."

Jefferson had had enough of the independence of the Judiciary and the separation of powers. He urged on the passage of an amendment to the Constitution, providing that federal judges might be removed by the President on an address from both Houses of Congress. Amendments along these lines were introduced in 1807 and 1808 and again during Madison's Presidency. But the life-tenure of the Federal Judiciary survived these and later attacks.

As late as December 1806, Jefferson was still hoping that his Presidency might end, despite the Burr affair, in peace and reconciliation, and that he might be able to hand on to Madison an undisturbed heritage of Republican supremacy. In his annual message to Congress he again referred to the prospects of a budgetary surplus, and had declined to curtail it by abolishing import duties and thus give "that advantage to foreign over domestic manufactures." Better to continue duties, the majority of which fell only on the rich, and apply them "to the great purposes of the public education, roads, rivers, canals, and such other objects of public improvement as it may be thought proper to add to the constitutional enumeration of federal powers. By these operations new channels of communication will be opened between the States, the lines of separation will disappear, their interests will be identified, and their union cemented by new and indissoluble ties." But the times were not such as to encourage much enthusiasm for the project of a national university. More interest was taken in the latter part of Jefferson's address, in which he spoke of the dangers of war and talked of "a steady, perhaps a quickened, pace in preparation for the defense of our sea-port towns and waters; an early settlement of the most exposed and vulnerable parts of our country; a militia so organized that its effective portions can be called to any point in the Union, or volunteers instead of them to serve a sufficient time."

Certainly the situation was menacing enough. With the outbreak of war between Great Britain and the Napoleonic Empire in May 1803, the whole series of problems relating to impressment, and interference with neutral commerce, had come to the fore again. As the struggle deepened and became, on the British side, one for national survival, the chances of much consideration being given to neutrals became ever more slender. In the first two years of the renewed struggle, while both belligerents still had fleets at sea, the Americans had little to complain of, and under the terms of Jay's treaty their trade, and especially their re-exports of colonial produce, rapidly grew.

But by 1805, both Britain's strategic interests and the permanent interests of the British mercantile marine appeared to be suffering from this lenity. By the decision in the *Essex* case, in July 1805, American commerce was again subjected to the rule of 1756 in its full rigour, and the pamphlet, *War in*

Disguise, or the Frauds of the Neutral Flags, published by James Stephen in October, advocated a scheme by which all neutral shipping should be regulated and taxed for the benefit of British navigation and the British war-effort; in the same month, the battle of Trafalgar made it possible for the most ambitious of such plans to be carried out. The possibility of balancing between the two naval Powers disappeared for the United States, when only one was left. On the other hand, to contemplate a direct conflict with England was hardly possible for a country where some sections were quite ready to expose the seaboard and its ports to their fate. The suggestion that a refusal to purchase British manufactures, and other measures of commercial coercion, would bring Britain to the point of abandoning impressment and the seizure of American vessels was scouted by southern Republicans. The trouble lay in the very existence of American maritime commerce, and in the determination of commercial elements to seize the opportunity of war for an unnatural expansion of the carrying trade:

"Shall this great mammoth of the American forest," shrieked John Randolph, "leave his native element and plunge into the water in a mad contest with the shark? Let him stay on shore and not be excited by the mussels and periwinkles on the strand."

In the following session of Congress a proposal to fortify New York produced another outcry from the old guard of Virginian Republicans. The fact that New York was unprotected was the best guarantee that there would be no war. John Eppes, Jefferson's son-in-law, declared: "If there is any principle which ought to be hooted at in a Republican government, it is . . . that to preserve peace we ought to be prepared for war."

Although Jefferson could command a congressional majority, the attitude of what was the original nucleus of his party was bound to have its effect.

Jefferson's attempt to use the method of commercial coercion was an ill-fated one. In April 1806 an Act was passed prohibiting the importation of certain British goods, but its coming into force was suspended while a special mission consisting of Monroe and William Pinkney tried to make terms in London. In December 1806 the envoys signed a treaty which followed closely on the lines of Jay's treaty, and so little favourable to American claims that Jefferson refused to submit it to the Senate. A British modification of their policy by the Order-in-Council of May 16, 1806, known as "Fox's blockade," did not mollify the Americans sufficiently to make them repeal the non-importation Act.

As the struggle in Europe progressed, both belligerents took further steps to prosecute their economic war. Napoleon's Berlin Decree of November 1806 marked the beginning of his "continental system" destined to exclude British manufactures from the whole of Europe. The British Orders-in-Council of January and November 1807 retaliated by prohibiting all trade with countries under Napoleon's sway except such as had gone through the British system of licensing, controls and tolls. By the Milan Decree in December 1807, Napoleon declared that neutrals accepting the British system would have their ships forfeited.

The dilemma before the Americans was less acute than might have been imagined, because the British system did in fact encourage a large amount of neutral trade, and the American merchants would gladly have gone on reaping its profits and accepting its controls. But the question of impressment was made more acute by the fact that British ships could, under Jay's treaty, make use of American ports for provisioning. This was brought to a head, in June 1807, by the attack of the *Leopard*, a British warship, on the American warship *Chesapeake*. The general indignation could easily have been utilized to secure a declaration of war, had Jefferson wanted it. But he was convinced that economic coercion would suffice, and, in December 1807, the Embargo Act was passed.

This unprecedented measure forbade the departure of any ships from American ports to foreign countries. It was indeed a self-blockade of the most rigorous kind, except in so far as smuggling to Canada and Nova Scotia, and the abuse of coastwise shipping, permitted its evasion. As such it did indeed inflict harm upon Great Britain, and still more upon her West Indian colonies. But although there have been differences of opinion as to its effectiveness, it was not a weapon which could bring Great Britain to heel, and the opening up of Spanish America to her trade provided some compensation after the outbreak of the Peninsular War in August 1808.

Jefferson—and he was not alone in this—consistently refused to admit the ultimate rôle of force in international relations, or the fact that by such standards the United States was still a minor power. In May 1806, when instructing Monroe upon the course to be pursued in England, he had written of the United States' potential naval strength (should France be willing to subsidize her) and had bombastically declared:

"We begin to broach the idea that we consider the whole Gulf Stream as of our waters, in which hostilities and cruising are to be frowned on for the present, and prohibited as soon as either consent or force will permit us. We shall never permit another privateer to cruise within it, and shall forbid our harbors to national cruisers. This is essential for our tranquillity and commerce."

It was to be a hundred and thirty-five years before an American President could effectively mark out a security zone in the waters of the Atlantic.

Nothing daunted, Jefferson had also begun to plan a new maritime confederation to impose American views of the freedom of the seas on Napoleon regardless of the rapid demise, at Britain's hands, of the Armed Neutrality of 1800. His great hope was the Emperor Alexander, for whom, according to the French minister in Washington, the American Government and particularly Jefferson had an "admiration which bordered on delirium." Indeed, Jefferson's occasional capacity for self-deception was perhaps never better illustrated than in his admiration for the Tsar, although it must be admitted that Jefferson was not the only liberal dupe of that curious monarch. His letter to Alexander of

April 19, 1806, in which he asked the Tsar to see that the forthcoming pacification of Europe incorporated a full recognition of the rights of neutrals at sea, was written in a tone which came oddly from an American patriot and republican.

"It will," wrote Jefferson, "be among the latest and most soothing comforts of my life, to have seen advanced to the government of so extensive a portion of the earth, and at so early a period of his life, a sovereign whose ruling passion is the advancement of the happiness and prosperity of his people; and not of his own people only, but who can extend his eye and his good will to a distant and infant nation, unoffending in its course, unambitious in its views."

Now Jefferson put his faith in the embargo. It was not merely a measure necessitated by the urgencies of foreign policy; it was to be the foundation of a new system. In a communication to the Tammany Society of New York in February 1808, Jefferson wrote:

"The ocean, which, like the air, is the common birthright of mankind, is arbitrarily wrested from us, and maxims consecrated by time, by usage, and by an universal sense of right, are trampled on by superior force: to give time for this demoralizing tempest to pass over, one measure only remained which might cover our beloved country from its overwhelming fury; an appeal to the deliberate understanding of our fellow citizens in a cessation of all intercourse with the belligerent nations, until it can be resumed under the protection of a returning sense of the moral obligations which constitute a law for nations as well as individuals. There can be no question in a mind truly American, whether it is best to send our citizens and property into certain captivity, and then wage war for their recovery, or to keep them at home, and to turn seriously to that policy which plants the manufacturer and the husbandman side by side, and so establish at the door of every one that exchange of mutual labors and comforts which we have hitherto sought in distant regions and under perpetual risk of broils with them."

But the transformation of an economy based upon foreign trade into a self-sufficient autarky could hardly be performed without deeply affecting private and sectional interests. And although it was true that industry flourished behind the protection of the embargo, this could not compensate for the losses suffered by the mercantile classes. The South remained loyal despite the loss of markets for its produce—a loss which contributed further to the decline of Virginia—and in the Middle States there was a balance of losses and gains. But New England revolted, Federalist separatism revived, and, in order to make the measure a reality, Jefferson was driven to enforce it by federal action, thus defying the whole States Rights basis of his party's political creed.

Jefferson continued for some time to cherish the illusion that all might be well. As late as August 1808, he was convassing the possibility that Great Britain might be reconciled with the United States; then if the war between Napoleon and Spain continued, the Americans might take Texas and the

Floridas. But the outcry that he was again sacrificing American interests to his predilection for France gathered strength. Inside the party, the dissidents headed by Randolph campaigned against Madison, Jefferson's choice as the candidate to succeed him—they were for Monroe; in New York another group supported Vice-President Clinton. Federalist victories in state elections showed the tide running against the Republicans. But the failure of the Federalists to come to terms with either group of Republican dissidents saved Madison. Even so, had Vermont and New York chosen their Presidential electors by popular vote, Madison might well have lost these states and with them Pennsylvania, and the election. As it was, the rise in the Federalist minority in the electoral college, from 14 in 1804 to 47 in 1808, did not represent the full extent of the swing. Jefferson's attempt to build up Republicanism in New England had collapsed, and it was clear that to continue the embargo would bring the Union close to destruction.

Jefferson strove to the last to preserve the embargo, and consoled himself for its diplomatic ineffectiveness by close attention to every sign of its protective effects. It had, he wrote to Lafayette, "produced one very happy and permanent effect. It has set us all on domestic manufacture, and will I verily believe reduce our future demands on England fully one half." But it became obvious that Congress would not wait for the end of Jefferson's Presidency before taking action. On March 1 the embargo was repealed; but the principle of economic coercion was not abandoned, since to replace it, Congress simultaneously imposed an Act of non-intercourse with England and France, to be lifted in favour of whichever first abandoned its measures against neutral commerce. Three days later, Jefferson stood at Madison's side while the implacable John Marshall administered to him the oath of office; it was Jefferson's last public appearance. At close on sixty-six years old, he was a private citizen again: this time for good.

Jefferson's second term of office as President had done much to destroy his popularity and influence, and congressional indifference to his wishes adequately expressed the feelings of most of the country outside his native state. It was indeed a melancholy paradox to which he had come. As Henry Adams put it:

"He had undertaken to create a government which should interfere in no way with private action, and he created one which interfered directly in the concerns of every private citizen in the land. He had come to power as the champion of States Rights, and had driven states to the verge of armed resistance. He had begun by claiming credit for stern economy, and ended by exceeding the expenditure of his predecessors. He had invented a policy of peace, and his invention resulted in the necessity of fighting at once the two greatest Powers in the world."

It was a long time before Jefferson's countrymen would be able to see his achievements in perspective and appreciate the greatness of the man at its true worth.

Chapter Ten

Elder Statesman
(1809–1826)

THE seventeen years of life which remained to
Jefferson after his retirement from the Presidency were years of declining physical strength but
undiminished mental vigour. Living at Monticello,
and never moving outside the adjacent counties, he
yet kept in touch with his surviving friends through
their visits and through correspondence, and even
opened up new interests and contacts both in the
United States and outside. These years were made
difficult by serious financial embarrassments—common at the time to most of the class to which Jefferson belonged, but added to in his case by his long
immersion in public affairs. Yet the preoccupations
which this caused him by no means diminished his
interest in politics or in the things of the mind. He
remained an indefatigable student, never too busy
to translate or see to the publication of new works
from France, or to exchange letters on the history
of the times through which he had lived, or on
more abstract topics. Such was the correspondence,
renewed in old age, after their long estrangement,
between Jefferson and John Adams. Jefferson's interest in the education of his grandchildren and
other young relatives brought him back to the
studies of his own youth, to mathematics and the
law; and in his own mind the great questions

of religion and ethics came finally to the fore.

Meanwhile, the fortunes of American democracy were not running smoothly. Under President Madison the various measures of economic coercion against the European belligerents proved ineffective, and the issues of impressment and neutral commerce remained unresolved. The growing western states and territories looked greedily upon the fertile lands of Upper Canada and with increasing animosity at their inhabitants, whom they accused of fomenting Indian resistance to the onward march of American settlement. In 1812 the western expansionists, profiting by the irritation over Britain's conduct at sea, forced the reluctant Madison into war with Britain. The war, and the economic and military measures which it brought in its train, inflamed once more the embers of New England Federalism. The hostility of the eastern states to the West had been manifested in the debates which had preceded the admission, as a state, of Louisiana, the first to be created out of the territories which Jefferson had acquired for the nation. Now the Union was being swung into an unnecessary war by the "war-hawks" of the West, and their southern accomplices who had been promised the Floridas as a balance for Canada! Federalist governors obstructed where they could. In spite of some individual exploits at sea, and of the New Orleans victory of Andrew Jackson—a man much mistrusted by Jefferson and one whose conduct in the Burr affair was rather equivocal—a victory won after peace had been signed in distant Ghent, the war brought little glory. Madison as President suffered the same

231

humiliation as Jefferson when governor of Virginia, in having to flee the capital; and Washington was burned to avenge the American treatment of York (the modern Toronto). The Peace of Ghent, the news of which caused the final collapse of New England disunionism, decided none of the issues over which the war was nominally fought; but the succeeding conventions settled the vexed Canadian boundary for much of its length and paved the way for the future peaceful co-existence of the two great North American nations. Shortly afterwards the high-handed actions of Andrew Jackson helped to secure the cession of the Floridas, and ended the other main source of trouble from the Indians and of friction with European powers.

President James Monroe, elected in 1816, the last of the "Virginia dynasty" and a much less considerable man than his predecessors, was fortunate in the timing of his accession to the Presidential office. The peace brought about a new national cohesion under the Republican party. Federalism became extinct, and the period of Monroe's Presidency acquired the name of the "era of good feeling."

It is true that the United States of the early 1820's was in many respects a different country from that of Washington's time. The shifting of the centre of gravity to the West could not be stayed. New states were added: Louisiana in 1812, Indiana in 1816, Mississippi in 1817, Illinois in 1818, Alabama in 1819, Missouri in 1821. Each meant a shift of power in Congress and in the Electoral College—the addition of Maine to the list of eastern states counted for little in the balance. But it was not only Federalist New England which lost weight in the national councils; the old-guard States Rights Republicans of Virginia were also outmatched.

The First Bank of the United States had been allowed to expire with its charter in 1811; but the confusion of post-war finance enabled the advocates of a new central bank to get their way and the Second Bank of the United States started on its eventful life. The new industries, built up in the shadow of war and embargo, demanded protection, and Hamilton's plan of a national tariff received posthumous vindication. Monroe came into office as sternly opposed to federal support for internal improvements without the sanction of a constitutional amendment as either Jefferson or Madison; but under pressure from western interests he weakened, and in the last years of his Presidency, and still more under his successor, John Quincy Adams, the federal purse-strings were loosened at last. The American democracy of the last years of Jefferson's life was a pushing, growing, diversified national community more interested in developing its heritage than in the old constitutional dogmas. The age of the Founding Fathers was drawing to a close.

It would have been surprising had Jefferson, in his rural solitude, paid equal attention to all these developments, although the root cause of most of them—the expansion to the West—owed as much to him as to any man. On some matters, Jefferson's prejudices remained unaltered. He was still contemptuous of paper money and ready to predict the downfall of Britain through her reliance upon it. Politically, the advent of the Second Bank of the

United States once more raised the question of its constitutional standing, and thus provided an important issue in the conflict between the western and southern states and the Supreme Court.

The Presidency of Madison saw a series of judgments in which the Court asserted its right to declare state legislation unconstitutional, and showed that it was likely to exercise this power to defend private and corporate property-rights under the cover of the Constitution's protection of contracts.

During the post-war depression, a number of states endeavoured to pass legislation for the protection of debtors and for curbing the operations of the Bank of the United States, whose mismanagement was largely blamed for the crisis. It was in connection with such legislation, particularly laws taxing the branches of the Bank, that the Court was called upon to decide the constitutionality of the Act to which the Bank owed its charter. The decision in the Bank's favour, given by Marshall in *McCulloch v. Maryland* (1819), and confirmed by his decision in *Osborn v. the Bank of the United States* (1824), marked an important stage in the judicial expansion of federal authority, since it put the Court unequivocally behind the Hamiltonian doctrine of the nature and extent of the implied powers.

The reaction to the decision in *McCulloch v. Maryland* was extremely vigorous, particularly in Virginia, where Spencer Roane, the head of the States Judiciary, was supported in his attacks upon it by Madison, by Thomas Ritchie, the editor of the powerful Richmond *Inquirer,* and by Jefferson himself. Jefferson held that the judiciary had once again thwarted the real will of the nation by standing for "consolidation" after the "Revolution of 1800" had clearly shown its preference for the "federal system." He went even farther than Roane by denying the latter's view (derived from the *Federalist*) that the judiciary would in the last resort decide the relations between the three constituent parts of the Federal Government. The fact that the judiciary was "unelected by and independent of the Nation" sufficed to condemn this view:

"The Constitution, on this hypothesis, is a mere thing of wax in the hands of the judiciary, which they may twist and shape into any form they please. It should be remembered, as an axiom of eternal truth in politics, that whatever power in any government is independent, is absolute also; in theory only, at first, while the spirit of the people is up, but in practice, as fast as that relaxes. Independence can be trusted nowhere but with the people in mass. They are inherently independent of all but moral law."

On the other hand, it should not be overlooked that Jefferson was here facing a new dilemma, since whereas in *Marbury v. Madison* the core of Marshall's offence had been his holding of an Act of Congress unconstitutional, what Jefferson was now objecting to was his failure to hold the Bank Charter Act unconstitutional also.

But the apparent inconsistency did not worry Jefferson, and he continued to use every occasion to denounce the dangerous doctrine that the Constitution had made the judges the final arbiters in all constitutional questions.

"How," he asked in his autobiography, "can we expect an impartial decision between the general government, of which they are themselves so eminent a part, and an individual State from which they have nothing to hope or fear? We have seen too, that, contrary to all correct example, they are in the habit of going out of the question before them, to throw an anchor ahead and grapple further hold for future advances of power. They are then in fact the corps of sappers and miners, steadily working to undermine the independent rights of the states, and to consolidate all power in the hands of that government in which they have so important a freehold estate."

The assertion of the Supreme Court's superior rights over the courts of the states themselves had been made by Marshall's colleagues in the series of cases arising over the Fairfax family's Virginia estates; and the state's point of view was eloquently expressed in three books by John Taylor of Caroline, published between 1820 and 1823. In *Cohens v. Virginia*, also decided in 1821, Marshall brought his own personal authority to bear in favour of the federal claim. Jefferson strongly supported the States Rights' point of view, and "cooked up" a letter to Taylor to be printed as an advertisement for one of the latter's books.

"The great object of my fear," wrote Jefferson to Roane in 1821, "is the federal Judiciary. That body, like gravity, ever acting with noiseless foot and unalarming advance, gaining ground, step by step, and holding what it gains, is ingulphing insidiously the special governments into the jaw of that which feeds them."

As the fight against the Court developed, it became clear that Jefferson, although more radical in his opposition to its claims than Madison, was himself not extreme enough for the real firebrands. Marshall's firm belief that Jefferson was the leading spirit in a campaign which he believed directed against the Constitution, and even against the Union itself, was quite unfounded, and is only testimony to the extraordinary lack of balance which the two great Virginians always displayed when confronting one another.

The real point was not whether the states of the South and West should disagree with the Court on these questions, but what they should do about their disagreement. The whole issue raised by the Virginia and Kentucky resolutions was alive again. The old proposal of an amendment to the Constitution limiting the terms of federal judges still seemed unlikely to go through, and Jefferson's proposal that Congress should specifically repudiate the doctrines of *Cohens v. Virginia* was also without sequel.

The question was whether the South, now in opposition, should adopt the tactics of the New England states during the war of 1812 and "nullify" federal legislation by refusing the co-operation necessary for its enforcement. The question of the Bank was an unfavourable one for testing the efficacy of such action, but the last two years of Jefferson's life saw the development of active opposition, in the South and West, to two new developments in federal policy—federal support for "internal improvements" and the protective tariff. Jefferson strongly condemned the method of constitutional construction used to justify the expenditure of federal revenues upon canals and roads within the confines of the states, and proposed that a new set of Virginia resolutions should be passed reasserting the doctrine of state sovereignty. But he would not go so far as to break with the Union. Only when there was no hope of avoiding "submission to a government of unlimited powers" should drastic measures be taken.

In stressing the need for the state governments to retain their full powers, Jefferson was not acting upon some abstract dogma of constitutional interpretation. It was a fundamental part of his democratic creed that smaller units in which the responsibilities of the individual citizen were clearer were more satisfactory than great agglomerations. He wanted to invigorate not only the state governments but also the counties into which the southern states were divided, and to subdivide these once more into what he called "wards"—equivalent to the New England townships. These wards, units of about six miles square, he compared to the hundreds of Anglo-Saxon England. But they were to have not only police powers, but also the care of the poor and of elementary schooling.

"The way to have good and safe government," he wrote in a letter of February 2, 1816, "is not to trust it all to one; but to divide it among the many, distributing to everyone exactly the functions he is

competent to; let the National government be entrusted with the defence of the nation, and its
foreign and federal relations; the state governments
with the civil rights, laws, police and administration
of what concerns the state generally; the counties
with the local concerns of the counties; and each
ward direct the interests within itself. It is by divid-
ing and subdividing these republics from the great
National one down thro' all its subordinations, until
it ends in the administration of every man's farm
and affairs by himself; by placing under every one
what his own eye may superintend, that all will be
done for the best."

In his autobiography written five years later, he
returned to the theme, concluding with a sentence
that commands a louder echo now than when it
was first enunciated: "Were we directed from
Washington when to sow and when to reap, we
should soon want bread."

Jefferson's hesitation over pressing the case
against the Federal Government too far was due in
part no doubt to the emergence of a weightier cause
of sectional dispute than any of the older ones—the
question of slavery. Were the new territories of the
Union to become slave states, thus further fortifying
the leadership of the old South, or were they to be
free states, which would mean preventing the
further extension of planter economy and the
society based upon it? If free states went on
being added to the Union, the slave states would
have less than the one-third of the Senate which
they required in order to exercise a veto on unfavourable legislation.

The issue first came to a head over the application of Missouri for admission to the Union as a state. The northern interests in Congress endeavoured to make a prohibition of slavery within its borders a precondition for admission.

Writing to John Adams in December 1819, Jefferson declared that all other political questions were put into the shade by this one: "The Missouri question is a breaker on which we lose the Missouri country by revolt, and what more, God only knows." In a letter in the following February, he declared that "at the gloomiest moment of the revolutionary war he had never felt equal apprehension." And in April he wrote that the Missouri question had re-aroused his dormant interest in public affairs: "This momentous question, like a fire-bell in the night, awakened and filled me with terror." Jefferson had regarded the raising of the question as a Federalist plot to create dissension in the Republican ranks, but by now he was writing in language which shows that he knew that much more than party was at stake. It is true that a solution had been found for the time being, by the admittance of Maine as a separate non-slave state to balance Missouri, and the decree that no further slave state should be admitted north of the latitude of Missouri's southern border. But he realized that the compromise could not be a lasting one: "A geographical line, coinciding with a marked principle, moral and political, once conceived and held up to the angry passions of men will never be obliterated." But as he confessed, the difficulties in the way of a real solution were formidable. Slavery should be abolished, but only if the free negroes could then be sent elsewhere, and so far no practicable method of achieving this had been suggested: "We have the wolf by the ears, and can neither hold him, nor safely let him go." Although Jefferson had been the author of the clause in the Northwest Ordinance which had first put territorial limitations on the expansion of slavery, he was not in favour of further limiting its geographical extent. The thinning out of the slave population by the spreading of it over a wider area was likely to improve the lot of the slaves, and to hasten their eventual emancipation. For the burden of emancipation would be more widely shared.

Since Jefferson had been so intimately involved in all the great questions of foreign relations which had emerged since the birth of the United States, it was natural that he should continue to be consulted over those which arose during his retirement. The most important of these in the years after 1815 was the question of the disposition of the Spanish colonies in central and south America which had revolted from Spain during the period of the latter's subservience to Napoleon, and which the Holy Alliance were now threatening to reduce to submission once more.

The United States took some time to formulate a national policy with regard to this question. Jefferson, as President, had cast speculative glances at Cuba and Mexico as well as at Florida, but for the rest had preferred not to hasten the course of events, lest Spain be succeeded by some stronger power. Under Madison, those interested primarily in Spain itself (where the United States was supplying the provisions for Wellington's peninsular armies) were opposed by the pro-French elements whose policy included vigorous co-operation with the South American rebels—a policy sustained by many Republicans on ideological grounds. The War of 1812 tended to narrow United States interest to the North American continent; and Great Britain entrenched itself strongly in the Latin American trade.

The years after the restoration of the Spanish Bourbons were years of great political confusion in South America, and at one time it appeared as though Spain would recover its hold. But from 1817 onwards, the insurgents began an almost uninterrupted succession of victories which only ended with the expulsion of the last upholders of Spanish power in January 1826. Four years earlier, Brazil had separated from Portugal and had become an independent empire. During these years, United States commerce with South America was becoming more important, and those concerned with it were doing their best to convince their fellow-citizens that Latin America was destined to follow in the peaceful and democratic ways of the United States.

Jefferson was somewhat sceptical as to the likely outcome of the hopes thus kindled. He believed that the inhabitants of these countries might well succeed in throwing off the Spanish yoke, but they had yet to prove their capacity for self-government: "The dangerous enemy is within their own breasts. Ignorance and superstition will chain their minds and bodies under religious and military despotism."

As late as December 1820, he was opposed to formal recognition of the independence of the Spanish colonies, on the ground that this would bring about a war with Spain, and perhaps with England too, if the latter thought that "a war would divert her internal troubles."

At the same time, a new complication had come into the situation through the growing signs of Russian interest in the New World. The Emperor Alexander, in whose liberal sentiments Jefferson had expressed such ill-founded confidence, was now the moving spirit of the Holy Alliance. And the Pacific Coast, where Jacob Astor's fur-trading vessels and the Lewis and Clark expedition had laid the basis for American claims to sovereignty, was now the scene of vigorous Russian activity. On the other hand, it became evident that any plans for Franco-Russian co-operation to suppress the revolts in Latin America would be looked at with disfavour by Great Britain, and Monroe made efforts in 1818 and 1819 to secure some co-operation from the British Government on this issue. But Castlereagh, whose policy still envisaged the restoration of at least the nominal sovereignty of Spain in her Empire, was in no hurry to welcome these approaches. For this reason the movement of the United States towards a more definite position remained slow, in spite of Monroe's strong personal sympathies. John Quincy Adams, Monroe's Secretary of State, was opposed both to Monroe's policy and to Henry Clay's alternative policy of all aid to the colonies short of war, and of forming a union of the two Americas as a sort of "counterpoise to the Holy Alliance." In the end, believed Adams, tyranny and colonial rule were bound to end everywhere, and the United States could afford to wait.

By the spring of 1822, the United States Government had come round to recognizing the insurgent Governments, lest it should find its influence supplanted by that of some European Power. There was also a good deal of alarm at reports that Great Britain was considering the acquisition of Cuba. Faced with this possibility, the Americans, true to their original policy, preferred to see Spanish rule continue.

It was in this atmosphere of mingled hopes and fears that the United States was called upon to define its policy when, in 1823, the success of French intervention in Spain seemed about to bring matters to a head, and when Canning's diplomatic approaches to Rush, the American minister in London, suggested that co-operation between Great Britain and the United States was now feasible.

Monroe forwarded to Jefferson Rush's reports of his conversation with Canning, and of the latter's proposal for a joint declaration by the two Governments, warning the other European Powers against attempting a reconquest of Spanish America, or transferring to another power Spain's sovereignty over any of her colonies. The President favoured accepting Canning's suggestion, and adding a declaration to the effect that an attack on Spanish America would be regarded as an attack on the United States, since it was to be presumed that the campaign against republicanism, if successful in the southern continent, would be extended to the north.

Jefferson's reply, on October 24, 1823, supported this view, even if the proposed declaration brought about war, which he thought improbable in view of Britain's strength at sea. He expressed himself willing to see Cuba independent rather than incorporated in the United States, since it could not be annexed without war with Great Britain. Since Jefferson regarded the question raised "as the most momentous" which had been offered to his "contemplation since that of Independence," he also took occasion to formulate the basis of American policy in more general terms:

"Our first and fundamental maxim should be, never to entangle ourselves in the broils of Europe. Our second, never to suffer Europe to intermeddle with cis-Atlantic affairs. America, North and South, has a set of interests distinct from those of Europe, and peculiarly her own. She should therefore have a system of her own, separate and apart from that of Europe."

Jefferson's letter directly links his earlier isolationist creed with the formulation of the Monroe doctrine. The President's message to Congress (December 2, 1823) was in fact delivered after Monroe had decided in favour of a separate policy by the United States rather than the co-operation with Great Britain envisaged in October. In spite of the differences between Great Britain on the one hand, and France and Russia on the other, it was felt that Great Britain was too far involved in the general European system for co-operation to be easy, and that the political ideals of her governing class were still far removed from those of American democracy. The dual principles of the Monroe doctrine—no further colonization of the American continent by outside Powers and no transfer of the sovereignty of existing dependencies—were in the main stream of Jeffersonian thought.

It would be a mistake to think of Jefferson in his last years as wholly, or even mainly, occupied with the great questions of national politics. His major interest during this period was not political but educational—the creation of the University of Virginia. His enthusiasm for the spread of education had never wavered. In January 1800, at the height of the contest between Federalists and Republicans, he had written to Joseph Priestley, the English scientist whose radical opinions had forced him to emigrate to the United States in 1794, of a plan for a University in upper Virginia "on a plan so broad, liberal and *modern,* as to be worth patronizing with the public support and be a temptation to the youth of other states to come and drink of the cup of knowledge and fraternize with us." In the same year, Jefferson wrote about his scheme to Du Pont de Nemours, who sent him a long memoir on public education based upon the French legislation of the revolutionary period.

After the interlude of his Presidency, he returned to Virginia full of schemes for an elaborate plan of general education. It was similar to that which he had advanced when a member of the state legislature thirty years earlier, but had been elaborated as a result of his correspondence with Priestley, Du Pont de Nemours and Destutt de Tracy.

The proposed structure of elementary, secondary

and higher education was embodied in a Bill introduced into the Virginia legislature in 1817, but it found little favour. Jeffersonian democracy thought more of economy than of enlightenment. Nevertheless, in the following year, the Virginia legislature made small appropriations for elementary education and for a University, and twenty-four commissioners, including Jefferson, Madison and Monroe, were appointed to prepare a scheme for the proposed University.

It was Jefferson who secured approval for locating the institution at Charlottesville, who designed the buildings, persuaded the legislature to spend further money, planned the curriculum and recruited staff. His correspondents in the Old World were called upon to assist in recruiting suitable professors who were still scarce in America: of the first seven appointed, only one was a native of the United States. Although Jefferson complained of the slowness of the proceedings and doubted whether he would live to see his work completed, the University of Virginia was eventually opened in March 1825; Jefferson wrote enthusiastically of his five professors from England and declared that he had never seen "a finer set of youths" assembled for instruction. The attainment of this ideal of a Virginian institution of higher education, freed from what Jefferson regarded as the cramping limitation of affiliation to a particular religious body, was, he believed, the crowning achievement of his career. When, in March 1826, Jefferson drew up his will, leaving to the University most of the second library he had collected, after being obliged to

247

raise money by selling the first to Congress, he gave directions that the inscription upon his tomb should describe him as "Author of the Declaration of American Independence, of the Statute of Virginia for Religious Freedom and Father of the University of Virginia." The scale of values which put these distinctions above those of President and Secretary of State was typical of the man who had written fifteen years earlier that he had never been able to conceive "how any rational being could propose happiness to himself from the exercise of power over others."

The end came to Thomas Jefferson, as to his old friend and rival, John Adams, on July 4, 1826, the fiftieth anniversary of the Declaration of Independence. Of the end of the American democracy whose destinies he had guided and whose aspirations he had voiced there was, and is, no sign.

Chapter Eleven
The Jeffersonian Legacy

THE fate of Jefferson in later American history has been the common one of great men. His name has been invoked to serve the limited interests of the moment, and that part of his activity or teaching which has not been found immediately useful has been jettisoned without regret. As has been seen, the span of years through which Jefferson lived and his own restless and eager mind precluded the building up of a completely consistent body of doctrine. For this reason it is not surprising to find him quoted on both sides of the same disputes. Thus in 1935, in his *The Jeffersonian Tradition in American Democracy*, Professor C. M. Wiltse declared that the philosophy of Franklin Roosevelt's "New Deal" was a "philosophy essentially Jeffersonian"; while in his book, *The Living Jefferson*, published a year later, James Truslow Adams denounced the "New Deal" as a move in the direction of dictatorship, deplored the Hamiltonian tendencies at work in it, and called upon Americans to rally against them in the name of Thomas Jefferson.

On the other hand, an equal distortion may arise from attempting to build up from Jefferson's sayings and writings a fully coherent academic philosophy and from forgetting his own predominantly practical and empirical bent. "I am not fond of reading what is merely abstract, and unapplied immediately to some useful sciences," he wrote to John Adams in 1816; and in a letter in the last year of his life, he declared that he revolted against "all metaphysical readings. These dreams of the day, like those of the night, vanish in vapour, leaving not a wreck behind. The business of life is with matter. That gives us tangible results. Handling that, we arrive at the Knolege of the axe, the plough, the steam-boat and everything useful in life; but from metaphysical speculations I have never seen one useful result." These views on philosophy in general are not without application to social and political philosophy. Jefferson was concerned with action and the reasons for action, not with founding a creed.

The real influence of Jefferson upon later American politics must be looked for in other directions. In the first place, there are the general assumptions underlying his whole outlook on politics which have been given a permanent vitality through the emotional appeal of the language in which he expressed them. In the second place, as a party leader, Jefferson provided an example of certain modes of political action which have come to form a part of the very texture of American democracy.

The history of American political parties after Jefferson's time made it almost inevitable that this should be the case. By the time of Monroe's Presidency, the Jeffersonian Republican-Democratic party had been so successful in making its general anti-aristocratic bias the touchstone of acceptability for anyone ambitious of elective office, that it had for practical purposes become the only political party in the country. Even so un-democratic a figure as John Quincy Adams could only work within its orbit. The process which can be followed in the development of Jefferson's own thought was at work in American society at large. The early emphasis on individual and minority rights weakened, and devotion to popular sovereignty increased. The business of the elected representatives of the people was to carry out the people's wishes. Not representation but delegation was the basis of the system. And it was the general levelling effect of this, alike in the political and the social sphere, that most impressed Tocqueville, whose visit to America took place within six years of Jefferson's death.

But beneath the general uniformity of political outlook, there emerged new divergences engendered by the rapid economic development of the country. Many of the features of Hamiltonian Federalism reappeared in the wing of the party which split off under Henry Clay's leadership, with the title of National-Republican and later of Whig. Against the largely big-business interests rallied behind Clay, and the protectionist, federally controlled "American system" which he propounded, there appeared under Andrew Jackson a new coalition, whose strength, like that of Jefferson's original following, lay in the agrarian South and among the less privileged elements of the urban population of the eastern seaboard. But Jacksonian Democracy was not identical in outlook with the party which Jefferson had led to victory. The emphasis on the individual, on the small man and his rights was there, but it was individualism with a difference. The new element is best represented by the word "enterprise"—it was equality of opportunity above all in the economic sphere that Jackson's followers were seeking. The stability which Jefferson had tried to bring about and fortify had vanished in face of the restlessness and acquisitiveness of the new age. Jefferson's constant concern for the creation and employment of an élite was abandoned when the right to office was incorporated into the doctrines of the party, and when the tasks of government were assumed to be within the capacities of every citizen.

Nevertheless, the Jeffersonian insistence that government must be controlled and that the people knew their own interests and were to be trusted was still the dominant note in American political life. Its effectiveness can be seen from the fact that the Whigs themselves could only hope to obtain power by adopting much of the Jeffersonian outlook, and so win for themselves another great stronghold in the still predominantly agrarian states of the northern Mississippi valley. Both parties were in fact Jeffersonian, and even the industrial protectionist wing of the Whigs could find justification for their doctrines in some of Jefferson's later reflections on the interests and destiny of his country.

In the next period of American history—the two decades before the Civil War—the Jeffersonian ideal received a still more vigorous challenge. As Jefferson had foreseen, the great question of negro slavery came to overtop all others, and under its impact both the major parties split. What was left of the Democrats accepted for a time the reshaping of Jeffersonian thought which Calhoun had carried through.

The natural-rights doctrine of the Declaration of Independence, with its inescapable corollary, the repudiation of human bondage, was sacrificed to the survival requirements of southern society. On the other hand, the technique which had served Jefferson so well, that of falling back on the rights of the states when the central authority was hostile, was taken up and redeveloped. The equality of the sovereign states of the Union was invoked to deny recognition to the equality of man.

On the other hand, many elements in the old Democratic party found a new home in the Republican party which arose from the débris of the Whigs. There they found a spokesman in Lincoln, but the association in a single party of Jeffersonian political theory with the economic and constitutional doctrines of Hamilton could not outlast the crisis which produced it. The aftermath of the Civil War and Reconstruction found both Republicans and Democrats once more national parties; but if the latter's formal pedigree as the heirs of Jefferson was the stronger, the agrarian elements in the Republican ranks were a guarantee against the development of a radically anti-Jeffersonian response to the demands of the new era.

To trace the history of party, and the permutations of the Jeffersonian doctrines, in the more recent periods of American history would take us too far afield. But the outside observer must always be struck by the lack of novelty in the solutions propounded for the new problems of the industrial age. The individualistic outlook so deeply rooted in an agrarian society remained characteristic of successive movements for reform. Where Europe accepted the fact of "bigness" in economic life and placed its hopes upon the ability of government to extend public control, the Americans preferred trying to create, artificially, the conditions of free competitive individualism, and spoke of huge agglomerations of financial and industrial capital in the language which Jefferson had found adequate for his denunciation of entails in colonial Virginia.

The periodic surges of democratic impulses—under Bryan, Wilson, Roosevelt—followed the course traced out by the Jefferson and Jackson revolutions. The Virginia–New York alliance—the alliance between the agrarian South and the urban masses of the East—forged by Jefferson and revived by Jackson, was still the inner core of Franklin Roosevelt's Democratic party.

The fact that the United States alone among the great industrial nations has clung to this belief, that the problems of industrialism can be solved within the framework of a competitive and individualistic society, that social justice is obtainable without public ownership, can be accounted for in many ways. But in the last resort their refusal to accept an *either/or* where freedom and equality are concerned is a reflection of an antithesis, permanently unresolved in the Jeffersonian mind.

Professor Wiltse has endeavoured to treat this problem by regarding the Jeffersonian tradition as a dual one containing both individualistic and socialistic tendencies, with "his characteristic position nearer to "social utilitarianism" than to the "individualism with which his name is apt to be associated." For "in affirming the best government to be that which governs least, Jefferson proclaims himself an individualist and commits himself to an economic theory of *laissez-faire*; but he declare also that the welfare of the whole`is the proper purpose of the state, and maintains the power of the Government to curtail the activities of the individual for the common good." It is not difficult to compile an anthology of Jeffersonian quotations to illustrate both aspects of this dual approach to the problem of politics. And it is no discredit to Jefferson that he failed to find a rational method of relating one set of objectives to the other; indeed, the history of democratic politics would seem to indicate that the problem is an insoluble one. The rights of the individual lead to majority rule; and majority rule, resulting inevitably in the disregard of the rights and interests of minorities, leads back to the search for individual guarantees. Jefferson's typically eighteenth-century attempt to avoid the necessity of giving a final answer, by asserting that a democracy could be entrusted with full powers, provided the people were "enlightened" by education, made little impression upon the next generation of American democrats.

Nevertheless, the Americans were compelled to explore the relations between public education and a democratic society in a very thorough fashion. This came about, paradoxically enough, through their rejection of one of Jefferson's other assumptions, the harmfulness of indiscriminate immigration. The successive waves of migration from different parts of Europe which marked the whole of the century succeeding his death meant that the Americans depended for their survival as a single nation upon the absorptive capacity of their society, and upon the rapidity with which the new-comers and their children could be brought to adopt the essential elements of the American outlook. And the importance which this conferred upon the whole problem of education, together with the continued emphasis on equality of opportunity, has made the unparalleled expansion of the educational system one of the most striking features of the American scene. It is only now that the increasingly complex demands likely to be made on American society in the future are becoming generally apparent, that consideration is again being given to the properly Jeffersonian conception of the selective element in such a system.

The contrast in Jefferson's constitutional doctrines between those he propounded when in opposition and those he acted upon in office is no less marked in the latest period of American government. The objects of government are still given equal weight with the modes of governmental action. The Jeffersonians in power under Franklin Roosevelt extended the federal powers just as Jefferson had done over Louisiana and the embargo; and now in retreat, the same democratic movement is beginning to rediscover the constitutional potentialities of the states.

A final dualism is apparent in the Jeffersonian legacy in the field of international relations. On the one hand there is the strong and persistent pacifist and anti-militarist tradition (Jefferson shared to the full the democratic illusion of the superior virtues of an armed citizenry). Wars are the products of the unjust and undemocratic imperialisms of the Old World from which the United States can stay aloof by self-isolation. The line of thought from Jefferson's embargo to the American rejection of the League of Nations and the neutrality legislation of the 1930's is a direct one. On the other hand, there is the belief in the sacredness of the American experiment and its right to the territorial room necessary for its expansion which led to Jefferson's Louisiana purchase and to his strong support of the movement for conquering Canada, to the seizure of Florida and, under the banner of "manifest destiny," to the expansion to the Pacific and the Mexican War under that good Jeffersonian Democrat, President Polk. This enabled Jefferson himself to put forward his startling doctrines as to the rights of the Americans in relation to the rivers upon which their territories abutted. "Nor is it in physics alone," he wrote just before the Mississippi crisis of 1795, "that we shall be found to differ from the other hemisphere. I strongly suspect that our geographical peculiarities may call for a different code of natural law to govern relations with other nations from that which the conditions of Europe have given rise to there."

The right of the Americans to the security of their country and their system was also more important

than the rights of other peoples and those general
principles of self-government of which they had
constituted themselves the upholders. Thus fearful
that the inhabitants of Louisiana might use political freedom to separate themselves from the United
States, Jefferson in 1803 argued in favour of giving
them an autocratic régime on the ground that they
were "yet as incapable of self-government as
children."

The right of the Americans to expand their area
of settlement whatever the consequence to the
Indians was of course axiomatic, and if Jefferson's
natural humanitarianism would have preferred a
peaceful solution to the problem, there was never
any question of a genuine conflict of rights. But the
demand for security could lead farther afield, particularly when the argument from geography was
as many-sided as it was for the Jeffersonians. Jefferson envisaged the Americans extending their sway
over the ocean as far as the Gulf Stream—which he
seems to have regarded as an extension of the
Mississippi. It was in similar view that Monroe
wrote to him in 1823 that he considered "Cape
Florida and Cuba as forming the mouth of the
Mississippi." Cuba was, rather strangely, to avoid
being swallowed up directly in the United States;
but the general assimilation of the islands of the
Caribbean and the whole of Central and South
America into the American security zone became
a conscious object of national policy with the enun-
ciation of the Monroe Doctrine, and a fact of politics as soon as American strength permitted. And,
as has been seen more recently, the doctrine is

capable of extension as far as Iceland at least on one side, and the Japanese mandated islands on the other.

It would be wrong to regard Jeffersonian democracy as merely a highly sophisticated form of imperialism. Jefferson always held that the real service of the Americans to the cause of freedom would be their example rather than their incorporation of other peoples; and the permanent rule of one people over another remained repugnant to the American mind. Indeed, the most lasting effect of Jeffersonian thought in this sphere has been the characteristic American unwillingness to face the fact of power, the American belief that the statement of correct principles is itself a policy, and an unreadiness to admit that political principles are themselves the product of time and chance.

The political fundamentalism of American democracy is not of course to be ascribed to the influence of Jefferson alone. It was the unavoidable consequence of the formative period of its history coming at the moment when the human spirit made one of its most daring leaps into the unknown by its attempt to find fixed principles for political and social life, not less self-evident than the physical laws of the Newtonian universe. Jefferson himself, with his constant emphasis upon the practical, was proof against the larger follies of the doctrinaire. In his comments upon French politics, extending from the eve of the Revolution to the height of the reaction under the restored Bourbons, he remained wedded to his original view that, for a people totally unused to self-government, complete democracy must pre-

sent dangers, and that the first essential should be
the establishment of the basic liberties from which
all others will in due time grow. Furthermore, it
was an essential part of his own idea of democracy
that governments should not run ahead of the ideas
of those whom they represent. This was the root of
Jefferson's differences with the physiocrats, for
whom, in other respects, he had so much sympathy.
"We both consider the people as our children," he
wrote to Du Pont Nemours in 1816, "and love them
with parental affection. But you love them as in-
fants whom you are afraid to trust without nurses,
and I as adults, whom I freely leave to self-
government." But it is possible to overstress Jefferson's readiness to fall in with the prevailing mood.
His abandonment of a wholly agrarian view of
America's destiny was not due simply to a surrender
to the popular desire to embark upon home manufactures.

It is true enough that the idea of the representative as delegate has been among the gravest
defects of American democracy in all ages, and that
this view of representative government can here
and there be justified from Jefferson's writings. But
the concept of public service and personal responsibility which Jefferson carried forward from an
earlier and more aristocratic age was a safeguard
against such a narrow view of the statesman's
function.

In the long run, Jefferson was an optimist about
mankind and its future. But the era of mass-move-
ments, popular tyrannies and inflamed national-
isms which the French Revolution inaugurated

did not seem to the mature Jefferson an improvement in every respect upon the previous age. In a letter written in 1813, Jefferson affirmed his weariness of politics and his preference for reading ancient rather than modern history:

"The total banishment of all moral principle from the Code which governs the intercourse of nations, the melancholy reflection that after the mean, wicked and cowardly cunning of the Cabinets of the age of Machiavel had given place to the integrity and good faith which dignified the succeeding one of the Chatham(s) and Turgot(s), that is to be swept away again by the daring profligacy and avowed destitution of all moral principle of a Cartouche and a Blackbeard, sickens my soul unto death. I turn from the contemplation with loathing and take refuge in the histories of other times, where if they also furnished their Tarquins, their Catilines and Caligulas, their stories are handed to us under the brand of a Livy, a Sallust and a Tacitus, and we are comforted with the reflection that the condemnation of all succeeding generations has confirmed the censures of the historian, and consigned their memories to everlasting infamy, a solace we cannot have with the Georges and Napoleons but by anticipation."

It is the voice of the eighteenth century—the voice of Thomas Jefferson.

For Further Reading

THE study of the career and influence of Thomas Jefferson can at no point be separated from that of the history of the United States as a whole. The best introduction to the subject and its bibliography is S. E. Morison and H. S. Commager, *The Growth of the American Republic* (3rd. ed., 2 vols., 1942).

The major source for Jefferson's own life is his own writings, particularly his correspondence. A definitive edition of the *Writings,* which is expected to run to fifty volumes, is now under preparation by Julian P. Boyd. Of earlier editions the best is that by P. L. Ford. (10 vols., 1892–9). The writings, other than the bulk of the letters, are conveniently accessible in the *Complete Jefferson,* ed. S. K. Padover (1943). Sections of the correspondence have been separately edited, particularly in the series of volumes by Professor Chinard dealing with Jefferson's French acquaintances.

The "official" biography is that by H. S. Randall (3 vols., 1858). Of more recent ones, the best are those by F. W. Hirst (1926) and Gilbert Chinard (1930). The *Living Jefferson,* by J. T. Adams (1936), is controversial; the biography by S. K. Padover (1942) has a useful bibliography. Jefferson's career up to 1776 is dealt with in *Jefferson: The Road to Glory,* by M. Kimball (1943). On his diplomacy, see the sketch by S. F. Bemis in vol. II of his *American Secretaries of State* (1927). On Jefferson's presidency, the standard account is still that in the first four volumes of Henry Adams's *History of the United States* (1889–90). A more favourable view of his foreign policy is taken by L. M. Sears in *Jefferson and the Embargo* (1927).

The following works are useful for their respective subjects: C. M. Wiltse, *The Jeffersonian Tradition in American Democracy* (1935); Adrienne Koch, *The Philosophy of Thomas Jefferson* (1943); J. C. Miller, *The Origins of the American Revolution* (1945); R. G. Adams, *Political Ideas of the American Revolution* (1922); *The Debate on the American Revolution* (ed. Max Beloff, 1948); C. A. Beard, *An Economic Interpretation of the Constitution* (1913), and *Economic Origins of Jeffersonian Democracy* (1915); N. Schachner, *Alexander Hamilton* (1946), *The Federalist* (ed. Max Beloff, 1948); V. L. Parrington, *Main Currents in American Thought* (3 vols., 1927); A. B. Darling, *Our Rising Empire, 1763–1803* (1940).

Jefferson, the Virginian, by Dumas Malone, the first volume of a projected 4-volume biography, appeared too late to be made use of in writing this book; so too did Marie Kimball's *Jefferson, War and Peace 1774–1786.*

Index

INDEX

Talleyrand-Périgord, Charles Maurice de, 170, 175, 216–17

Taylor, John, of Caroline, 177, 236

Texas, 217–18, 227

Tocqueville, Alexis de, 104, 108, 251

Townshend, Charles, 36

"Townshend" duties, 36, 40–1

Turgot, Anne-Robert-Jacques, 80

Turner, F. J., 213–14

Vans Murray, William, 180

Vattel, E. de, 24, 55

Vergennes, C. G., Comte de, 102

Victoria, Queen, 4

Virginia Association, 40

Virginia (Commonwealth), institutions of, 71–8, 112, 117–18, 123; decline of, 227; education in, 246–7; University of, 247–8

Virginia (Province), 3, 13–18, 26–9, 46; laws of, 23; legislature of, 25–6, 34–6, 39, 43, 50–2; economic and social structure, 26–9; religion in, 26; opposition to Great Britain in, 34–6, 39–41, 49, 53–4; conventions in, 53–4, 59, 63

Virginia resolutions, 177–9

Voltaire (François-Marie Arouet), 7

Walcott, Alexander, 85

Walker, Thomas, 83

War of 1812, 231–2, 242

Washington, D.C., description of, 188–9

Washington, George, 32–3, 40, 50, 61, 78, 85–7, 89, 114–15, 121, 127, 130, 132, 138, 142, 147–8, 167–9, 171, 182, 189–90, 193

Watt, James, 6, 19

Wayne, Anthony, 159–60, 162

Wellington, Arthur, Duke of, 242

Western lands questions, 32–3, 74, 82–5, 98, 118, 160, 195

Westward movement, 158–9, 195, 202–3, 232–3

Whig Party (American), 251–3

Whisky rebellion, 155

Whitney, Eli, 6, 164

Wilkinson, James, 218–19

William and Mary College, 18, 78–9

Wilson, James, 56, 70, 124

Wilson, President T. Woodrow, 10, 190, 240

Wiltse, Prof. C. M., 249, 254–5

Wythe, George, 19–20, 23–4, 73, 75–6, 84, 122

X, Y, Z correspondence, 170, 174

271

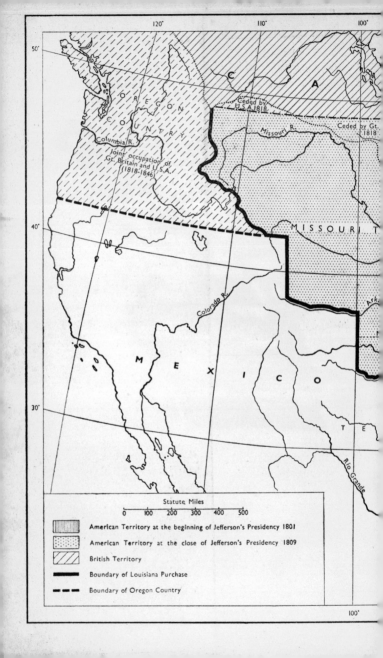

Statute Miles

0   100   200   300   400   500

American Territory at the beginning of Jefferson's Presidency 1801

American Territory at the close of Jefferson's Presidency 1809

British Territory

Boundary of Louisiana Purchase

Boundary of Oregon Country